Our Connectional Church

Our Connectional Church

The Hopeful Future of the PC(USA)

Gradye Parsons

WESTMINSTER JOHN KNOX PRESS
LOUISVILLE • KENTUCKY

Contents

Foreword

> "Bring out your dead," cries the man pushing a cart in *Monty Python and the Holy Grail.*
> "I'm not dead," asserts a potential corpse.
> The collector of the dead says, "He's not dead. I can't take him."
> "He will be soon," says the man carrying the body in question.
> "I'm getting better," says the man hoisted on the shoulder of doomsayer. "I feel fine."

In some ways, this sounds like the conversation that swirls around the Presbyterian Church (U.S.A.), but we're far from dead, and we might even look forward to feeling better.

Today, we find ourselves at a potential inflection point in the long history of the Reformed tradition. We are five hundred years past Martin Luther's nailing of Ninety-five Theses to the church door in Wittenberg. We are three hundred years past the creation of the first Presbyterian synod in the Americas. Our oldest seminaries have celebrated two hundred years. We are one hundred years beyond the 1910 World Missionary Conference in Edinburgh, which is often seen as the beginning of the ecumenical movement, and more than fifty years have passed since the number of mainline Protestants peaked in the United States.

Today we are arguably in a post-Protestant era. Neil Gorsuch is the only Supreme Court justice who identifies as Protestant and the first mainline Protestant to join the Supreme Court since 1990. The two most dominant expressions of Christianity in America today are mediated salvation and transactional theology. The former results in religious hierarchy and the latter manifests itself in everything from the prosperity gospel to media-driven megachurches.

In bold contrast, our Reformed tradition offers a very different theology, relying on the strength of grace, faith, and the authority of Scripture. This understanding manifests itself in inclusive community, connected ecclesiology, and an imperative for social justice. It is a witness that is still very important in today's world. All these are reflected in Rev. Gradye Parsons's gift of this book to the Church.

From the beginning, American Presbyterians have recognized the need to care for those who serve the Church. At the inaugural meeting of their first synod, in Philadelphia in 1717, American Presbyterians established the Fund for Pious Uses. The first award from the fund to an individual was to the widow of the Rev. John Wilson of New Castle, Delaware. As we celebrate our tricentennial, we also celebrate the thirtieth year of the modern benefits plan that was created after reunion of the northern and southern Presbyterian denominations in 1983. That plan has now been updated for a new era.

With sound theology, constant learning, mutual accountability, and a deep desire to listen to others' stories, we have learned that we must embrace change and adapt. The Board of Pensions has learned that the best stewardship is that which looks ahead to determine how to best plan for future needs. Simply grasping tighter to what we already hold is neither wise nor faithful.

The board has been reforming and refining ever since the widow Wilson received a grant of three pounds Sterling to help raise her children. Beginning on January 1, 2017, the board began offering a flexible and more affordable benefits plan for church workers and their dependents. Since then, over four thousand new members have been enrolled. We continue to evolve, offering broader educational opportunities through Board University, providing economic and spiritual support to young ministers, promoting wellness through the Call to Health and enlivening the Body of Christ by supporting those who serve the Church.

The Board of Pensions chose to sponsor this book project in celebration of its tricentennial because we do indeed take the long view. Our projections suggest that membership in PC(USA) will stabilize and a decade from now may even begin to grow. Our faith tells us that God is not finished with this particular expression of Christ's Church. It is likely that someone on our rolls today will be getting a financial benefit in the twenty-second century. With the perspective of a three-hundred-year history, it is easier to look beyond the horizon of the next few years.

As part of a long-range planning effort, we have developed projections to help us understand where the PC(USA) may be going. What we discovered will be of interest to all those who are concerned about the future of our beloved denomination. But before we look ahead, it is important to understand where we stand as a denomination right now.

First, we wanted to look at the makeup of our congregations, the unit of measure with which all Presbyterians most easily relate. We examined the 2016 data reported by the Office of the General Assembly in Part II-A of the minutes of the 222nd General Assembly.[1] The numbers at first do not look promising. Total congregations have declined from over 10,000 in 2012 to 9,453 in 2016. Of the 9,453 congregations listed in the 2016 statistical report, 5,396 (57 percent) have membership of fewer than 100 with an average membership among that group of only 45. Another 1,265 (13 percent) report membership between 101 and 150. That leaves 2,792 (30 percent) with membership at 151 and above.

Church Size	Total Members	Average Church Membership
Fewer than 100	242,371	45
100 to 150	149,136	118
Over 150	1,090,517	390

Here is where the story begins to change. Those larger congregations average 390 members and operate with an average budget of over five hundred thousand dollars. Almost all of these congregations have installed pastoral leadership, a

1. https://www.pcusa.org/resource/minutes-general-assembly-2016/.

building, and enough resources to pursue an active mission. Our surveys suggest that they typically have five or six employees.[2] This is the predominant experience of congregational life for members of the PC(USA). If one asks, "Where do Presbyterians go to church?" rather than, "How are our congregations doing?" this prototypical larger church is the answer. In fact, 74 percent of our members, some 1.1 million people, belong to one of these 2,792 larger churches.

At the other end of the spectrum, new worshiping communities have brought life and innovation to our communion. The Presbyterian Research Services reports 348 new worshiping communities were active at the end of 2016. Research Services says that new worshiping community leaders self-report an average of 50 regular attendees per community.[3] If all regular attendees were counted as members, that would be approximately 17,400 additional people, or just over 1 percent of total membership.

Therefore, what we see are three predominant groups of churches:

- Small congregations of 150 members or fewer dominating the number of congregations but representing only 26 percent of membership, which, for a variety of reasons including demographic factors, are unlikely to grow in significant numbers.
- Emerging ministries, which are very important theologically and add richness to the life of our communion but still represent a very small number of members.
- That group of relatively larger churches that often enjoy multiple pastoral leaders and are often growing.

In the stories and conversations that follow, you will see signs of vitality in long-established and emerging ministries; in churches small and large; and with people and in settings that are diverse in every respect. A few things hold all of them together:

2. Board of Pensions survey 2013.
3. Presbyterian Mission Research Services, "1001 NWC Leaders Report," February 2017, https://www.presbyterianmission.org/wp-content/uploads/1001-NWC-final-report-with-appendices.pdf.

being connected as Presbyterians, being concerned about congregational community, being committed to social justice.

Can the Presbyterian Church grow, both in terms of numbers and vitality? We think so. It is unlikely that PC(USA) has saturated any large market. In Charlotte, with one of the highest concentrations of Presbyterians in the country, growth seems synergistic rather than competitive. Four of the five largest churches are growing larger, on average increasing membership 11 percent from 2012 to 2016 with an average 2016 membership of 2,565. The largest African American congregation in Charlotte is C. N. Jenkins Memorial with 834 members, growing at 8.4 percent in membership over the same period.[4]

Examples of growth are not limited to Charlotte by any means. In 2014, the last year for which we have full data, of the churches with over 1,500 members in Dallas/Fort Worth, Nashville, Greenville/Spartanburg, Raleigh, Greensboro, Minneapolis, Tampa, Chicago, and New York, all increased in size from the prior year.[5]

Further analyzing the 2016 Office of the General Assembly data, we explored some scenarios to inform our long-term planning. We ran twenty-five years of projections. Based on current trends, our assumption was that membership of churches with 150 members or fewer, which constitutes 26 percent of Presbyterians, will continue to decline at a rate of 10 percent per year. We then ran a number of scenarios, based on observations of membership dynamics in larger churches, which assumed that those churches in which the other 74 percent of Presbyterians are members grew at rates between 0 and 3 percent. The results are perhaps surprising.

Depending on how one reads the data, one could make a strong argument for the 1 percent growth scenario among the larger churches. Assuming that the majority of departures spurred by theological controversy are behind us, a sampling of the largest churches suggests that growth between 1 and 3

4. https://church-trends.pcusa.org/church/search/.
5. Office of General Assembly 2014 statistical report source data.

percent is not unreasonable where there is stability and strong leadership. This indicates a bottoming out of membership at approximately 1.4 million and modest expansion beginning somewhere between 2025 and 2030. Even if there is zero growth among the larger churches, our membership bottoms out at approximately 1.125 million

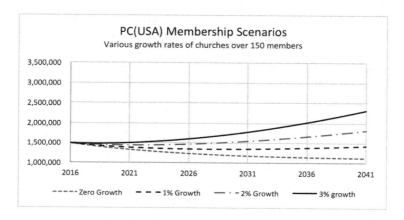

We need to find ways to support the vital ministries that exist in our smaller congregations and lift up as witness those forms of emerging ministries that have sprung forth. But for PC(USA) membership to actually grow, we must focus substantive resources of time, talent, and treasure in those areas where critical mass makes growth most achievable. We should support dynamic congregations and presbyteries where the highest concentrations of Presbyterians already exist.

According to the Pew Research Center, the region that stretches from Washington, DC, to Dallas is generally more culturally supportive of religion in general, and Christianity in particular, than other regions of the country.[6] This also has been an area of the country with in-migration and steady population growth, consistent with some of the membership gains already noted. Those concentrations are reflected in a review of our Presbytery membership:[7]

6. http://www.pewforum.org/religious-landscape-study/#geography.
7. PC(USA) Minutes, Part II-A 2016, 222nd General Assembly.

Top Ten Presbyteries by Membership

Greater Atlanta	35,360
Grace (Dallas)	31,754
Charlotte	31,505
National Capital	29,814
Chicago	28,949
Philadelphia	28,514
Pittsburgh	27,673
New Hope (Raleigh)	27,235
Salem (Winston-Salem/Greensboro)	23,778
Coastal Carolina	23,601

The Board of Pensions has already begun to reflect these realities in its hiring patterns. Grouping Texas as one geographic region and North Carolina as another, we now have church consultants to provide a physical presence in all of the ten largest presbyteries. Four of the ten are in North Carolina, which is the primary reason the board chose that state for its Lilly Endowment–funded pilot project, "Healthy Pastors, Healthy Congregations."

By various measures, the church we know and love is disappearing, emerging, and thriving, all at the same time. In my conversations throughout the denomination, many who have experienced dramatic reduction in numbers at the congregational and presbytery level tend to see mission in the world as communal action within the denominational structure. In contrast, those in growing congregations tend to understand mission as located in the local context. Both are undoubtedly true and they aren't, or don't have to be, mutually exclusive.

Rev. Gradye Parsons is in a unique position to bring insight to our life together in this denomination. As former Stated Clerk of the Presbyterian Church (U.S.A.), Gradye has led us in denominational matters for eight years. As a mid-council leader, Gradye has worked with congregations of every sort and size. As a minister of several congregations, Gradye has experienced the joys and frustrations of life in the parish. Gradye writes with keen insight and great joy as he chronicles what is right and good within our connected communion.

Gradye helps us celebrate the connections through which we support each other and reinforce missional impact. We have abundant resources: amazingly talented and faithful people, strong financial agencies that serve the Church, and a PC(USA) corporate balance sheet of $525 million in net assets to support mission and program.[8] God has provided all that we need to live out a strong witness to the world in the name of our Lord, Jesus Christ.

It is easy to be disheartened by the decline of mainline Protestantism in the United States, but when we look closely, the reality is much more complex. Numbers don't tell the whole story, as faithful disciples labor in fruitful ministries and make a real difference in the quality of life in their communities all across the nation and around the world. Our members lead for-profit and not-for-profit organizations that are transforming our communities, our country, and the world. They are nurtured spiritually by the community that has been gathered in Jesus' name. You will see all this in the experiences Gradye shares.

The PC(USA) is far from dead. In fact, there is realistic hope that we might even get stronger. To make that hope a reality, with prayer and the work of the Spirit, we must focus resources on connecting healthy tissue to healthy tissue. This book lifts up many exciting ministries and celebrates the connections between us. It shows the dynamism of our theology as we work together to fulfill the sixth great end of the Church: the demonstration of the Kingdom of Heaven to the world.

The Rev. Frank Clark Spencer
President, Board of Pensions of
the Presbyterian Church (U.S.A.)

8. PC(USA), a corporation, audited financial statements, 2016.

Acknowledgments

I want to give my deepest thanks to the Rev. Frank Spencer, who asked me to write this book. It was the best retirement transition project a Stated Clerk ever had. I want to thank my wife, Kathy, who transcribed some of the longer interviews. She found their stories very inspiring. I want to thank seminary professors, ministers, and presbytery leaders for granting me interviews and engaging in thoughtful conversation. My journey took me to Seattle, Atlanta, Charlotte, Philadelphia, Chicago, Knoxville, Austin, and San Antonio. Special thanks goes to my editor, David Maxwell, who was patient, firm, encouraging, and helpful. There would be no book without him. Most importantly I want to thank God for that day I walked into a Presbyterian church. It began a call on my life and a journey with many wonderful friendships.

1

The Presbyterian Aquifer

Thanks to the generosity of the Presbyterian Board of Pensions, I was able to visit a number of congregations and leaders across the United States and take a snapshot of our church today. I recently ended a long period of service at the national church level that kept me in touch with the broader church, but this project gave me the opportunity to step back from governance issues and soak up some of the rich ministries happening across the denomination.

The main quest with this project was to discover the nature of the connectional life of the Presbyterian Church (U.S.A.). That nature takes many shapes and forms, depending on personality, geography, and role. For some people it is a very deep connection to their congregation, and for others it may be a set of colleagues. For some the connection is to the ministry in which they are involved, and for others it is to Reformed theology.

As I reflected on the conversations I had, a common linkage to a Presbyterian ethos seemed to appear. This ethos, made of several parts, operates like an aquifer—an underground layer of water-bearing permeable rock, sand, or gravel. The Ogallala Aquifer sits underneath a huge portion of the central United

States. One person may draw water from it to irrigate crops. Another person may tap it to wash their car. We see different applications of the same source material.

I am going to describe some of the elements in our Presbyterian aquifer. This discussion is not meant to list all the components. I hope you will talk with your Presbyterian circle about what you believe should be included.

GRACE AND GRATITUDE

A sincere attempt is under way to make "Grace and Gratitude" the byline of the Presbyterian Church (U.S.A.). It would be for Presbyterians what "God is still speaking" is for the United Church of Christ. If that attempt was successful, I would be pleased. "Grace and Gratitude" is a three-word summary of the Reformed understanding of faith. Because of the grace initiated by God for us, the undeserving, we respond in gratitude by worshiping God and living holy lives. You could say it is the antidote for works righteousness. One of my best moments as a teaching elder was when I was able to help a recovering fundamentalist understand how important *ex nihilo*, the concept that God created the world out of nothing, was to understanding the grace of the God who acts first in our salvation story.

Despite the best efforts, Presbyterians have not quite arrived at the place where "grace and gratitude" rolls off their tongues, yet they use other language that has its roots in grace and gratitude. To say, "I have a call to ministry," is not unique to Presbyterians. That all are called to a vocation by God is bedrock Reformed theology. However, the use of the term "call" is so much a part of our Presbyterian lingo that we don't appreciate the theology it states. For in saying, "I was called," we are conveying that the One or someone outside of me initiated this ministry, this moment, or this space. The answering of that call is the gratitude.

Grace and gratitude is the modus operandi of the Presbyterian Church. It implies humility and stewardship. God so loved the world (grace), and I will love my neighbor (gratitude). We are called to worship (grace) and go out to serve (gratitude). I would go so far as to say that most of the struggles and crisis in our denomination or in our congregations have taken place when we have drunk from some other well.

QUESTIONS

A recurring theme from the many interviews I had in preparing this book is a deep appreciation that we are a denomination that welcomes questions. The purpose of the historic Reformed emphasis on education was originally so that people could read the Bible for themselves and not depend on others to choose what parts to read to them. The result is that women and men are able to ask and answer questions about faith individually and as a community, which creates a dynamic interchange of ideas, hopes, frustrations, and possibilities. "Being free to ask questions is a strong appeal for people who become part of Northwood Presbyterian Church," stated its pastor, Rev. Traci Smith.

The fact that we have a Book of Confessions is a testimony that we are wrestling with the questions of what it means to be a disciple of Jesus Christ. Even without the historical background material of the Confessions, you can understand the context in which they are written. The Confession of 1967 clearly speaks to the racial conversation of the 1960s in America. Yet Belhar was added because the reality of racism is still before us.

The pastors interviewed told me stories of people becoming part of their congregations because they were places where people could ask questions. It may be one of our most useful evangelism tools. Being able to ask questions gives people permission to try out their new Presbyterian clothing. It also gives congregations new insights about how to be a Christian in this day and age. Rev. Lisa Lopez emphasized that when Christ Presbyterian Church gathers for Bible study, they want to ask questions. "They are dealing with real issues in their life, and they want to be able to ask what it all means."

At the 2016 General Assembly in Portland, many people took their meals at a diner near the convention center. On the last Friday of the assembly, a friend asked a waitress if they were going to stay open late to take care of the many attendees who would be hungry after a long day and too jazzed to go to sleep after all the debates. The waitress replied that they were trying to talk their boss into staying open late. "We want to stay open late enough to welcome the Presbyterians and then turn on the closed sign. We want to be able to sit down with them and talk about the conversations the assembly has had all week."

To be able to ask questions and seek answers as a community of faith is not just a theological issue. It is also a pastoral one. When practiced well, our congregations allow for serious questions about God and faith in the difficult times of individuals' lives. In the face of great loss, who does not wrestle with doubts? A denomination that encourages questions also creates a space for emotions. Presbyterians are accused of being the frozen chosen. As a minister and in the interviews for this project, I see a church that may get stuck in some traditions but still attends to the real dynamic of the everyday life of its members.

Many of us like some certainty in our faith. That certainty allows us to build a solid foundation of understanding and gives us a rock to cling to in the storm. The sheer weight of all that Presbyterians have written about faith and Reformed theology is a foundation itself. But by and large, all of those books, articles, and sermon manuscripts were trying to answer the question of what it means to be a Presbyterian person of faith—a question we all ask ourselves every day.

STRUCTURE

Presbyterians love to complain about our church structure. In fact, complaining about our church structure is a very common well in this aquifer of our ethos. People say they don't like meetings, the Book of Order is too restrictive or too lax, and who are they to make that decision? The "they" depends on where you sit in our polity. "They" could be the session, presbytery, synod, or General Assembly.

I have been privileged to serve in all of the councils of the church. I have sat through endless committee meetings. I have heard the groans of people who equate all of this effort with wasted time. But I was reeducated during this project.

For those who come out of less structured traditions or out of traditions with a rigid hierarchy based on being a male, our structure is the water of life. The opportunity to serve the church as a woman minister or a gay or lesbian minister is something that never happened in their former denominations. This is not to say it is easy in the Presbyterian Church (U.S.A.). However, it is possible because as a body we have made decisions to change our structure to make it so. The decision to open ourselves to the leadership gifts of all of our members was made after endless committee meetings and debates in the councils of the church. For years, the structure voted no. But the very fact that the structure allowed us to ask the question and to vote on the answer made the change possible.

Our structure does take a lot of energy to maintain. That energy is not wasted when our polity serves its purpose to help us be the faithful church of Jesus Christ.

LEADERSHIP

Many people would say that the reasons Presbyterians are often leaders in their community is because of the socioeconomic circles that make up Presbyterian congregations. There would be some truth to that, but it would not be the whole truth. Creating leaders and nurturing leadership is in every droplet of water from this Presbyterian aquifer. A thinking faith that expects service in the community is going to birth leaders. Those leaders are known in their community and are drafted as civic leaders, charitable board members, and the go-to women and men when groups want something done. Today, there are thirteen U.S. senators who are Presbyterians and thirty-five Presbyterians in the House of Representatives. While not all of these are from the PC(USA), it does reflect a rather out-of-proportion sample of leadership for our size.

Having leadership that is elected is in our polity. Teaching elders, ruling elders, deacons, trustees, and moderators are all duly elected by group decision-making. We even elect our nominating and search committees. I think it can be said that the ones electing are giving leadership, too. Our commitment to group decision-making brings everyone into the leadership arena. Making decisions about who leads, how they lead, and where they are leading a faith community invites everyone into thinking as a leader.

The gift of the office of ruling elder with its ordination is a unique role in our leadership. It transforms what could be seen as a board of directors' role into a spiritual one. The councils of the church are not charged with just making decisions but with making decisions with serious spiritual discernment. The role of the ruling elder is further respected by the requirement that all councils beyond the session have equal numbers of teaching and ruling elders. This schooling in leadership creates leaders who are trained to listen to others and the Holy Spirit, giving the church leaders who have varied gifts and deep commitments.

COMMUNITY INVOLVEMENT

What do John Calvin, John Witherspoon, John Glenn, Elizabeth Dole, and Condoleezza Rice have in common? They all believed their faith had to be lived out in the public square. This is not a by-product of Reformed Theology, it is its *chief* product. Presbyterian community involvement includes food pantries, hospitals, Habitat houses, homeless shelters, immigrant services, community gardens, rural aid, early education programs, and civil rights work.

In 1986 a group of Presbyterian women in the Synod of Mid-America and another in the Synod of Lincoln Trails camped out on the doorsteps of Senators Nancy Landon Kassebaum of Kansas and Richard Lugar of Indiana. The women demanded that the senators do something about U.S. support for apartheid in South Africa. Our government policy at that time was called "constructive engagement," which did very little to influence South African leaders to stop persecuting the black-majority population. The two senators ended up writing a joint letter to then President Reagan saying they would no longer support this policy. Subsequently, with their support, the Senate adopted the Anti-Apartheid Act of 1986.

John Calvin secured sewers, schools, homes, and trades for the many immigrants in Geneva, Switzerland. The gratitude we express toward God is to be lived out in all the aspects of our life. One of the most direct measures of the church's faith is found in the Confession of 1967:

> The church disperses to serve God wherever its members are, at work or play, in private or in the life of society. Their prayer and Bible study are part of the church's worship and theological reflection. Their witness is the church's evangelism. Their daily action in the world is the church in mission to the world. The quality of their relation with other persons is the measure of the church's fidelity.
>
> (9.37)

To measure the church's fidelity to God by the quality of individual members' relationships with people outside that congregation is setting a very high bar. If we are going to wear God's grace out in public, we cannot conceal it from others. In Matthew 25 Jesus is very clear that God cares about God's children who are hungry, thirsty, estranged, imprisoned, and ill clothed. We are not to see them as problems. We are to help them as though we are directly helping God.

Presbyterians may argue on how we live our faith in the public square. We may take different sides of the policies that help people. But the aquifer of our ethos pumps up gushers when we take God's call to serve others seriously.

EDUCATION

I have been asked many times where the Presbyterian schools are. Why don't you do grade school and high school like other traditions do? There are some Presbyterian schools today, and there were many more in the past. The answer I usually give is to point out the nearest public elementary school and say that is one of our schools.

On average, Presbyterians are highly educated. It was Calvin's charge that we all be able to read the Bible on our own, but that is only a part of it. Presbyterians believe education is for everyone. An educated society is a healthy society. However, our sense of our own education can become a stumbling block. "Our intellect can become a prideful idol," shared Rev. Pen Peery of First Presbyterian Church in Charlotte. "At our best, we should communicate our intellectual resources and message humbly." In the early, struggling years of the University of Tennessee, the faculty had consisted of so many Presbyterians that other faith traditions complained. There were six historical Presbyterian colleges in the nearby Appalachian Mountains. There is also a tradition of mission schools that predated public education in rural counties. This situation is not unique to Appalachia. In the westward journey of the Presbyterian Church into such places as Ohio, Indiana, and Illinois, schools were often built before churches. Presbyterian pastors were often the teachers. Education has always been seen as empowering people to be able to look at the world with a wider perspective. We have tried to never mix education with conversion. Education has been one of our most principled ministries and has served as an aquifer to benefit a much wider community than our own.

PREACHING

Proclamation of the Word is a Presbyterian core ethos. Presbyterians do not have the market cornered on good preaching, although we do have high standards for it. I take delight in listening to retired ministers in their seventies and eighties tell me excitedly how they communicated a vital part of the lectionary text. I wrestle with my humility when someone quotes something I said in a sermon long ago.

Our education standards for ministers of the Word and Sacrament are high. They have been the source of more than one church split. We have had infamous heresy trials. We expect our preachers to know their Bible, Reformed theology, and the world around them. In my seminary days, we were taught to have very little of our self in the sermon. It is not uncommon now to hear more self-reflection and sharing of common struggles. Preachers who were once placed on a pedestal are now expected and honored when they are more firmly placed on earth.

The traditional marks of the true church are

> The Word of God is truly preached and heard,
> the Sacraments are rightly administered, and
> ecclesiastical discipline is uprightly ministered.
> (F-1.0303 *Book of Order*)

Though the traditional understanding of "heard" has been to receive and to follow, I want to offer another aspect. Though all Protestant traditions have good preachers, I believe there is an especially Reformed understanding of what happens in a sermon between the preacher and the congregation. A Presbyterian congregation knows that they are not just recipients of the Word but that they have an obligation to think through on their own both the text and the message. The best compliment a Presbyterian preacher can get is to have someone say, "You gave me something to think about," or "I had never thought about that text like that." The best sermon experience in worship is not a voice speaking to sponges but a heart and mind engaging other hearts and minds. In this way, the aquifer of this ethos is fed continually.

WORSHIP

In chapter 2 I tell my story of engaging Presbyterian worship for the first time. Since that day I have been in many PC(USA) congregations from Barrow, Alaska, to San Juan, Puerto Rico. I have gathered with congregations in marvelous sanctuaries that would make Solomon envious. I have celebrated the sacraments in basements, sheds, tents, and business buildings. It would be reassuring for seminary professors to hear that all worship is in the same format and of the same quality, but it is not.

What is a consistent part of the Presbyterian ethos is that worship is important. Congregations continue to bring the best of their resources and talents to their worship. In the high liturgical congregations there are bulletins of serious lengths with many places for the congregation to give common voice to their love of God. In the simpler liturgical congregations, there is usually space for individuals to give of their talents. Ministers of Word and Sacrament take seriously their responsibility to plan worship. Whether it is high or simple liturgy, planning is essential. One of the contributions of the liturgical renewal movement is that worship planning is more than a good sermon and a good choir anthem. Proclamation of the Word includes all of worship.

> God's gifts of Word and Sacrament establish and equip the Church as the body of Christ in the world. The mission of the one, holy, catholic, and apostolic Church flows from Baptism, is nourished at Lord's Supper, and serves to proclaim the good news of Jesus Christ to all. In the same way, the Church's ministry emerges from the font, arises from the table, and takes its shape from the Word of the Lord. Therefore **the worship of the triune God is the center of our common life** and our primary way of witness to the faith, hope, and love we have in Jesus Christ.
>
> (W-1.0107: *Worship and the Church*
> [emphasis added])

The truth is the Church's. The worship of God is the center of our common life and where our deepest relationships to each other are nourished. We belong to each other because we belong to God. This ethos that acts as an aquifer is a gift from God as God calls this church into being and nurtures it by the Holy Spirit. In life and in death, we belong to God.

2

The Local,
Worshiping Congregation

The connectional life of the PC(USA) is realized for most Presbyterians in their local congregation. This is not a new or profound statement. What may not be as appreciated is the integration of Reformed theology that distinguishes the worship of a congregation and creates community. The Reformed understanding of the role of the Holy Spirit in worship, the importance of the congregation at the table, the community promises made at baptism, our collective confessions, and the centrality of the Word craft a unique community. And you and I are gracefully called to be a part of it.

When I was in college, a group of my friends talked about a fun Sunday school class at a suburban Presbyterian church. The group talked me into going, but I was not that impressed with the class. However, I decided to stay for worship. It was a life-changing decision.

I had never before had my heart and mind so engaged in a worship service. Everything about it was thought out and done well. The congregants sang with a mixture of reverence and joy. The pulpit was front and center. The table was stationed on the floor so that table and Word seemed one. What looked like an out-of-place sundial I soon discovered was the baptismal fount.

Church had been part of my life since birth, anchored by a small, mainline church in town with my father's childhood friends and cousins and a country church a few hours away filled with my mother's childhood friends and cousins. My grandmother presided at the little organ in that country church. She would play my favorite hymns when we visited. Like most church folk, I grew up with pastors of mixed abilities and gifts. I overlapped with two sets of preacher's kids. We tortured them in abundance, and they gave it equally back to us. Both my parents taught Sunday school at one time or another. I was the leader of our youth group and a regular summer church camp attendee. I was no novice to the idea of church.

Early college days were not church days for me. There were too many new adventures to be had, too many weekend distractions. But after the death of my church organist grandmother, something started tugging at me. A friend told me about his faith. A couple of propitious books jumped off the bookstore shelves at me. Prayer regained its daily place in my schedule. Considering it was the early seventies, I could have easily taken up the path of finding God in the glorious mountains near campus. But my faith story had always been a part of a larger community story. I didn't know what I was looking for in a community. College Bible studies were interesting and often populated by pretty girls, while the Christian jock scene seemed to make Jesus a personal trainer.

It was not a very intentional search. I was more of a wanderer on an unseen road that I would later come to believe was God's grace. It led me to a congregation I had never been a part of and the Presbyterian Church I had only known from afar.

The fact is that three out of five people sitting in Presbyterian Church (U.S.A.) pews are just like me. I was not baptized in your font. I did not grow up with your traditions. I had your sacraments but served up in different ways. We had different kinds of leaders. Outsiders think all mainline Protestant denominations are basically the same. They are the same the way any two families are the same. They may look alike on the outside, but they differ a lot.

Presbyterian worship has as its traditional marks the centrality of the Word and the two sacraments of the baptism and the Lord's Supper.

> God's gifts of Word and Sacrament establish and equip the Church as the body of Christ in the world. The mission of the one, holy, catholic, and apostolic Church flows from Baptism, is nourished at Lord's Supper, and serves to proclaim the good news of Jesus Christ to all. In the same way, the Church's ministry emerges from the font, arises from the table, and takes its shape from the Word of the Lord. Therefore the worship of the triune God is the center of our common life and our primary way of witness to the faith, hope, and love we have in Jesus Christ.
>
> (W-1.0107)

The Rev. Dr. Ted Wardlaw of Austin Seminary says, "Reformed worship is theologically inherently communal at its best. There is a given going back to our beginning that the sacraments are not something that we watch but something we participate in together. It is not a sacrament because the minister is there, but because the people are there."

This common life, this communal life, is fed by different aspects in the worship service. The role and placement of the common prayer of confession emphasize John Calvin's view of our human sinfulness. The placement of the prayer of confession before the sermon and not before the Lord's Supper is a statement of how important we acknowledge the Word is to us.

Dr. Anna Carter Florence says, "There is something about confessing all together that lifts you above your individual failings. Then the affirmation of my forgiveness leads me to make amends with the grace that I have received."

These worship elements, these rituals, weave the theme of the service together, but they also connect the people. Singing from common hymnbooks (known by color as much as by name), the Lord's Supper shared by ruling elders, and the basic call-and-response—"This is the Word of the Lord. Thanks be to God."—creates a community both catholic and apostolic but also uniquely Reformed.

The Holy Spirit is at work, too. Dr. Kim Long reflects, "We pray for the Holy Spirit to come down and open us to preaching, and we pray for the Holy Spirit to come down on the elements of the Lord's Supper and the people."

> Lord, open our hearts and minds
> by the power of your Holy Spirit,
> that as the scriptures are read
> and your Word is proclaimed
> we may hear with joy what you say to us today.[1]

Just as God is in community in the Godhead, the *our* and *us* in the preceding prayer are claiming a common experience in the word proclaimed. It is not preached at but encountered with the people.

> Liturgy shapes individuals, to be sure, but its primary form is communal. The community is prior to any individual's membership in it. Liturgy is an exercise of that community, the Body of Christ, and is its central demonstration to the world. Acting in God's name, the community invites us into itself to hear the gospel, to receive baptism, to come to the table to receive the bread and wine, and then sends us into the world to serve. Because it is a communal activity, it requires a logical progression. . . . In the Gathering Rite, we step out of our worldly preoccupations and into the assembly where we acknowledge God's claim on us. We confess our failures to live in terms of God, abdicate the egocentrism into which we continually fall, and proclaim God's victory over sin. We hear the Word, stories of God's acts in former times and find our new identity in terms of what

---

1. From *A Service of Word and Table 1*, © 1989 The United Methodist Publishing House. Used by permission. All rights reserved.

God has done and promises to do. Knowing we have no strength but God's strength, we come hungry to the Table to be fed and strengthened in order to follow Christ into the world. Then, fed and healed and restored by grace, we are sent to be the Body of Christ in the world. All of these acts are possible in the faith community alone.[2]

The Rev. Dr. Martha Moore-Keish teaches theology at Columbia Theological Seminary. She shared two personal stories that made the connection between sacraments and community.

The sacraments are opportunities to connect. My daughter Miriam was born in Atlanta in 1997 and baptized in Central Presbyterian Church. We moved away for seven years and then came back, rejoining Central. I have this memory of her coming to worship with our friends, the Forneys. As I sat in the choir at the front of the sanctuary, I could see Miriam sitting with them in the balcony. During the Lord's Supper, she came down with them to the table, passing the font where she had been baptized seven years earlier. The Forneys weren't part of Central when she was baptized, and yet as part of the extended family of the church, they helped raise this child through promises made and kept in other congregations. It was the movement through the body from font to table that spoke to me of this deep connection we experience around the sacraments.

Again, at Central, this time more recently, my younger daughter, Fiona, and I returned to regular worship at Central after participating for several years at another church where my husband was on staff. One Sunday Fiona was sitting by herself in the congregation, while (once again) I was in the choir. I watched her looking forlorn, still trying to feel at home in a place where she had not been regularly attending for several years. It was hard to be separated from her in that moment. As the prelude began, I scanned the congregation, noting who was present that day, and I was

---

2. "Continuing the Tradition of Reformed Liturgy and Music," *Call to Worship: Liturgy, Music, Preaching and the Arts* 38, no. 2 (2004–2005).

glad to see my friend and colleague Rodger Nishioka in his usual place in the balcony. The service went on, and during the first hymn I looked around again, and discovered that Rodger had disappeared. *How odd*, I thought. But a verse later, he reappeared—next to Fiona on the ground floor. For the first time that morning, she smiled. They made origami cranes together during the sermon. During communion, they came forward together to the table, and then passed by the font—where Rodger took a handful of the cranes they had made and dumped them in the water.

Again, a member of the extended church family took my beloved child into his care, accompanying her to the table, and although he had not been present at her baptism, he recognized it and remembered the promise congregations make to help raise and care for all.

These stories are repeated in different ways across the Presbyterian Church (U.S.A.) and also in synagogues and mosques. Worship is a communal experience. There are particular elements in Reformed worship that create unique bonds. My wife and I were part of the Anchorage Presbyterian Church in Louisville, Kentucky, for almost sixteen years. The minister, Rev. Dee Wade, and I are the same age. I was invited to preach my last Sunday there. I paid Dee a compliment that others might not understand, but I knew he would appreciate it. I said that I had sat in the congregation with the same folks week after week and year after year. I knew most of them and their stories of struggles, fears, failings, hopes, joys, and successes. On many occasions, the sermon they preached with their witness in worship was as powerful as the word coming from the pulpit. Dee understood that compliment, as most ministers with long tenures would.

The Rev. Il Sun Kim of the Korean Presbyterian Church of Knoxville relates how each congregation is not an independent body any more than any one cell in the human body can exist without the others. "God called us to be his body and to be Presbyterian." The calling to be Presbyterian is also a calling to be in community with other Presbyterians.

In Jesus Christ, the Church is called to be a royal priesthood, giving glory to God in worship and devoting itself to God's service in the world. Worship is a collective activity of the people of God and an expression of our common life and ministry. It demands the full, conscious, and active participation of the whole body of Christ, with heart, mind, soul, and strength.

(W-2.0201)

3

Beyond the Congregation

Beyond the congregation, the Presbyterian Church (U.S.A.) lives out its connectional life in presbyteries, synods, and the General Assembly, and through agencies and institutions they have created. That connectional life reflects a commitment to communal decision-making, ordered ministry, and the mutuality of congregations.

The communal decision-making is done through debate and discourse between ruling and teaching elders who serve in these bodies as equals. It is done through elected commissioners, so not every Presbyterian is participating in the decision-making. Participants experience the input of people in different congregations and different contexts, and often with different concerns. The Rev. Veronica Cannon served as a committee moderator at the 222nd General Assembly in Portland. She observes, "I learned how broad and diverse the life of the church is. I heard a variety of voices and grew a deeper appreciation for how we govern ourselves." Though the impact of a General Assembly can be large, the numbers of individual Presbyterians who experience it are few. There is a disconnect in that situation. When I was the Stated Clerk of the General

Assembly I would often be asked to speak a pastoral or prophetic word about a national issue. I knew I was bound to say only what was within General Assembly policy. I also knew that many Presbyterians would read the statement and have no idea that a General Assembly policy was behind it. It is a challenge to be a connected church when many are unaware that we are connected.

One of the ways we are connected is through ordered ministry. We decide together where and what ministry needs to be done and who will be doing that ministry. It is fairly clear to a Presbyterian congregation that the presbytery participated in selecting their minster. As each year passes from its charter date, it is less clear to the congregation that its presbytery had a role in the birth of the church. The extent to which a congregation feels connected to the larger PC(USA) often depends on when and how a congregation first gathered. Rev. Lindsay Armstrong is executive director of new church development for the Presbytery of Greater Atlanta. She told a story about spotting a van displaying the name Chin Presbyterian Church, USA and the PC(USA) seal. She had never heard of the congregation, so she followed the van out of curiosity. When the driver stopped at a store, she followed him inside and engaged him in conversation. He told her, "We were Presbyterians in Myanmar. When we migrated to the United States we said, "Now we are Presbyterians in the USA, so we named ourselves Chin Presbyterian Church USA." Armstrong then helped them begin the process of joining the presbytery. The Chin church wanted to be connected.

In 2010 the Presbyterian Church (U.S.A.) adopted a major revision to the Book of Order, the first major revision since reunion in 1983. One new sentence was added that described a reality that had always been present in the church but needed to be emphasized.

> The congregation is the church engaged in the mission of God in its particular context. The triune God gives to the congregation all the gifts of the gospel necessary to being

the Church. *The congregation is the basic form of the church, but it is not of itself a sufficient form of the church.* Thus, congregations are bound together in communion with one another, united in relationships of accountability and responsibility, contributing their strengths to the benefit of the whole, and are called, collectively, the church.

(G-1.01 [emphasis added])

The Rev. Dr. Paul Hooker describes the importance of that sentence:

I like to think of this paragraph in light of Paul's metaphor of the body of Christ in 1 Corinthians 12. Each congregation, like each part of a body, represents the whole body. If I wave my hand, it is not merely my hand waving ambiguously in the air but my whole being recognizing the presence of another or seeking recognition from another. What happens to a hand or a knee affects not only the hand or knee but the whole body. If you want to test this, try breaking your foot and see if your whole body does not suffer through the pain and the recovery process.

A congregation has the gifts needed to be a congregation, in the same way that a hand or knee has the anatomical architecture to perform its function. But that function, while essential, carries its greatest meaning when it is part of the whole: a hand may grasp, but that grasp has meaning only when an arm reaches out at the behest of a brain that seeks to grasp the hand of another in friendship or hold another's hand in love. A congregation has all the gifts needed to be the church, but the greatest form of its ministry is realized only in the organic connection to the rest of the church—indeed, in connection to the whole people of God—as the whole church seeks to participate in God's transforming work in Jesus Christ. In the end, congregations are at their best when they live in mutual relations of accountability and responsibility with one another, giving of themselves and receiving from each other, so that collectively we are the Presbyterian Church (U.S.A.).

Such a church is one that reflects the theological reality of the triune God, ever three and yet ever one, bound in such relationship as to be ever united even while ever distinct. Such a church is one that lives out the historic Nicene commitment to the unity of the Church of Jesus Christ. This notion that congregations are more nearly the church when they are in relationships with each other is the foundation for our notion of the councils of the church (Form of Government, ch. 3), and thus underlies not only our sense of what a congregation is but also how we understand the whole church. It also underlies our view of the property of the church, and thus the importance of G-4.0203 (the property trust clause): because we are organically connected to one another, as the parts of the body are organically united. Loss or injury to one is loss or injury to all, and strength and health of each part contributes to the health of the whole. Finally, it underlies our use of per capita apportionment as a shared source for the funding of the mission the church is called to fulfill: in the same way that each part of the body shares in the complex work of the whole body, so each part of the church is needed to share the complex work of the whole church.

In an era in which many congregations, like the individuals who are part of them, increasingly believe that their responsibility ends at their own doorsteps, I think this notion is critically important and represents a gift to the Church as a whole.

The American pull-yourself-up-by-your-own-bootstraps mythology goes against the idea that my congregation needs your congregation to be complete. Some of the large congregations in the PC(USA), with their many staff positions and vast facilities, seem to be self-sufficient islands. Further investigation reveals that their ministers learn to lead in smaller congregations and many members were nurtured in other, smaller congregations first. They are in partnerships with other Presbyterian congregations in mission and church planting. Curriculum is purchased from the denomination, and their youth groups benefit from national gatherings. The ministers are usually in some sort of national or local lectionary preaching support groups.

Rev. Lisa Lopez, Rev. Shawna Bowman, and Rev. Shannon Kershner serve very different congregations in the Presbytery of Chicago. Their stories highlight the connectional nature of the PC(USA).

Lopez was in a small youth group in her church in Puerto Rico. One day the spouse of a pastor from another Presbyterian congregation visited them and encouraged them to come to a presbytery youth retreat. Lisa had no idea there were so many other Presbyterian teenagers. Her gifts were affirmed by the faith community, and she attended Princeton Seminary with the aid of scholarships from the seminary and national offices of the PC(USA). After serving as an assistant minister in Northern Ireland she was called to Christ Presbyterian Church in Hanover Park, Illinois. Hanover Park has become a haven for people escaping violence in the inner city of Chicago and many people from Latin America. The once all-white congregation now has families from ten different nations.

Lopez says she encourages members to pass the peace in their own language, creating a mini-Pentecost on Sunday mornings. She feels the presbytery has her back as she faces challenges. For example, the congregation received notice that its tax-exempt status was to be revoked because of a missed filing. "I was trained to be a pastor, not a lawyer," explained Lisa. "I turned to the presbytery staff, and they connected me right away with the right people. The front steps of the church had deteriorated to a point where the city ordered the church to fix them or close the building. I didn't see how my fifty-two congregants were going to be able to raise that money and pay their own bills." With advice from presbytery, encouragement, and some donations from individuals from other Presbyterian congregations, the large steps were repaired and a vital ministry was preserved.

Bowman is the pastor of Friendship Presbyterian Church. Unlike Lisa, Bowman has no building challenges since Friendship rents space in the Norwood Park Metra train station and does not want to own a building. Friendship is the merger of two congregations that both sold their buildings. The merger was the result of conversations nurtured by the Presbytery of Chicago. The sale of the buildings created resources for ministry and opportunity for two congregations to really become one. The congregation's mission is to create relationships that transform lives. Through storytelling the congregation is learning to tell their faith stories. Members were encouraged to record their version of "This I Believe," and that recording was shared in worship.

Friendship is a creative place where Reformed worship is described in different ways. "Our call," says Bowman, "is to find out what works and report it out." Bowman also participates with other presbytery members in Creation Lab, a collectively shared studio where people can nurture their creative side. Bowman explains that ministers can get burned out, and the hope of this space is to allow them to rediscover their creative energies.

Fourth Presbyterian Church sits grandly in the heart of downtown Chicago. "Some people enter the building and are surprised it is a church," reports Kershner. She grew up in Waco, Texas, where her father Jimmie was pastor of First Presbyterian Church. Shannon spent summers at Mo-Ranch, the large conference center in Kerrville, Texas. As with Lopez, it was a Presbyterian professor at Trinity University in San Antonio who urged her to use her gifts in ministry. Kershner tried out ministry as an intern at St. Phillips in Houston and then headed to Columbia Theological Seminary. From there, she returned to Texas and served two different calls. Then she was called to Black Mountain Presbyterian Church in North Carolina, which sits down the road from the Montreat Conference Center. In 2014 she was called to be the pastor of Fourth. Kershner is active in Next Church, an organization in the PC(USA) that seeks to strengthen relationships between healthy leaders and between congregations. Members share innovative ideas and best practices for ministry.

Kershner and I were part of a worship conference at Mo-Ranch in 2013. She was the daily preacher, and I was the daily Bible study leader. The conference focus was that year's Advent text. We divided our labors. Kershner preached on the gospel, and I taught the Isaiah texts. I got to know her father and the many other Texan folk who had influenced her life. I include this story to make the point that the minister of the very large Fourth Presbyterian Church in Chicago is the sum of the collective places and people of the PC(USA) that encouraged and taught her along the way. This is as true about me as it is any other Presbyterian minister. We ministers are the result of the communal discernment by the church, guided by the ordering of ministry, and we serve mutually dependent congregations.

Revs. Lopez, Bowman, and Kershner have all found ways to be connected in the PC(USA). But there are occasional challenges for congregations to make those connections. Rev. Bowman observed that congregations that are in survival mode rarely have any energy left over to relate to other congregations. Rev. Danny Murphy, executive presbyter in the Presbytery of the Trinity, says, "The connectional nature used to be so strong that you hardly had to promote unified giving [where local churches destine part of their budget income to the national church for mission]. Now I have to take church leaders out to lunch to convince them to give." Rev. Mark Verdery, general presbyter of Providence Presbytery, reflected "that the majority of Presbyterians used to be cradle Presbyterians. Many people who are elected as ruling elders and deacons aren't aware of the connectional nature of the church beyond their own congregation. We dropped the ball on officer training and are reaping the effects." In reality, 60 percent of the people in the PC(USA) are not cradle Presbyterians, which is also true for most of the historic mainline denominations. Rev. Tim Reynolds of Second Presbyterian Church, Knoxville, Tennessee, addressed this challenge of educating the congregation about the basics of Presbyterianism by preaching a series of sermons over a summer that were basically an adult confirmation class.

Rev. Jan Edmiston, co-Moderator of the 222nd General Assembly, shared that congregations often resent the time their minister spends away from the congregation doing presbytery work and receiving continuing education. However, when people do get away, either pastors or congregational members, they are nourished and bring good ideas back to their congregation. The equipping piece never ends.

Rev. Donnie Woods, general presbyter of the Presbytery of Charleston-Atlantic, is developing relationships between congregations by gathering them into "neighborhoods." Outside of requiring two meetings a year, the neighborhoods are allowed to develop their own sense of community. Rev. Bruce Ford, former executive presbyter of Trinity Presbytery, reports that the twenty-one African American congregations are very connected and model that connection for the rest of the presbytery.

Rev. Eliana Maxim, associate executive presbyter in Seattle Presbytery, relays a story about John Knox Presbyterian Church. The new pastor at John Knox, Rev. Chris Pritchett, went on a presbytery-sponsored trip to Colombia, where they have a mission partnership with the Presbyterian Church in Colombia. As the delegation saw mission in a very different context, it helped them think how they might apply some of this mission in their Seattle context. Maxim says, "The power of taking people out of their context and shaking them up a little can empower them to see their ministry differently." John Knox was sharing its space with Misión Hispana, a congregation of Central American immigrants. As soon as Chris returned to Seattle he called the pastoral leader of Misión Hispana and suggested doing a weekly joint Bible study together. They then started finding ways to bring the two congregations together. After several months the session of John Knox voted to nominate the Misión Hispana pastoral leader to be a ruling elder, to sit on session with a focus on Spanish-language ministries. The Misión Hispana community is now attending membership classes with plans to join John Knox in 2018. In the meantime, the presbytery is partnering with both groups to provide the pastoral leader with an online theological educational program with the hopes that he can eventually be ordained and serve alongside the pastoral staff at John Knox. This is an excellent example of a mid-council nurturing relationships among its churches.

I asked Rev. Sallie Watkins of Mission Presbytery, Rev. Cathy Ulrich of Eastminster, and Rev. Ruth Santana-Grace of the Presbytery of Philadelphia what a good day in their presbyteries looks like. Following are their replies.

For me, a good day around Mission Presbytery involves generosity, camaraderie, creativity, and community. Good days like that happen more often than not, fortunately. At a recent presbytery meeting, the presbytery youth attended and led us in two energizers during my report. We heard from Tony De La Rosa, then interim director of the Presbyterian Mission Agency in Louisville, about all the latest from the Presbyterian Mission Agency. We also had an hourlong workshop with Mark Yaconelli on the power of storytelling.

It was wonderful to hear the sanctuary abuzz with conversation and laughter as people shared stories with each other. During worship, we heard a barn-burner sermon from one of our newest and youngest pastors. And we collected an offering for "Mo in the Valley," a program where Mo-Ranch took its leadership (and at least one of its cooks) to the Rio Grande Valley to provide camp for children who could neither get to nor afford a week at Mo. The offering was well over two thousand dollars.

For me, the best part happened after the meeting, where people I hadn't met came up and hugged me, saying that they'd been a commissioner to the presbytery meeting and that it had been a fabulous experience for them. More than one pastor has told me that elders on session are now fighting over who gets to come to the next meeting. That's how I think going to presbytery should be!

(Sallie Watkins, Mission Presbytery)

A good day in Eastminster is one of sharing faith, hope, love, trust, and witness to Jesus Christ. The moderator of the presbytery and the co-Moderator of the GA led a discussion of racism and our role as people of faith. Participants filled the room. The conversation was so challenging and rich that there is a plan to have another conversation at the annual DiscipleFest. Akron-area pastors, in response to the situation in Charlottesville, are planning a presbytery-wide antiracism and nonviolence training. A relationship with the National Evangelical Synod of Syria and Lebanon, begun two years ago, is continuing with churches contributing to the work with refugees, and a trip is planned in 2018. Plans are being made to use the proceeds from the sale of our camp to promote ministry in churches.

(Cathy Ulrich, Eastminster Presbytery)

A good day in the Presbytery of Philadelphia reflects the threads of a colorful tapestry bringing together differing dimensions of our life. A good day looks like a reflection of our call to be a people of the impossible—a people of resurrection hope.

When we began talking about the city's three hundredth anniversary, we quickly became committed to not simply making it a celebration of the past but of an awareness of our call and relevance for the future. We are raising three hundred thousand dollars for eight initiatives addressing children and education, breaking the school-to-prison pipeline, and encouraging restorative justice. We have less than ten thousand dollars to go, and we are one month away. I am deeply moved because presbyteries don't tend to raise extra dollars outside of emergencies. This looks like a good day in our life as it has rallied small and large congregations as part of a larger covenant community.

A good day in the life of our presbytery is collaborating with partners to breathe new possibilities into existing ministries. In the past three years, we have developed a Ministry and Leadership Incubator. In partnership with Princeton Theological Seminary, we recruit six seminarians who serve three congregations. In teams of twos, these students serve these congregations while also being part of a monthly cohort to discuss areas of ministry of interest to them such as non-for-profits, administration, creative spaces, and so on. Our time with them reminds us of how God continually calls up new leaders.

A good day is reflected in our gatherings with smaller groups. This past week, we hosted a barbecue for emerging leaders at my home. The energy throughout the house was palpable. What a privilege to serve these saints as they breathe freshness into our life as a presbytery. We recently did a similar gathering for inquirers and candidates. These gatherings allow for relationships to be built among peers without an agenda.

A good day in the life of our presbytery is gathering for courageous conversations on issues of race and bias and worshiping together as we cling to the light at a time when darkness and the sounds of -isms of all kinds are framing the public discourse and sphere.

(Ruth Santana-Grace, Presbytery of Philadelphia)

Rev. Gordon Raynal, stated clerk of Foothills Presbytery, says that the time of institution-building is over. This statement is echoed in numerous books and articles about all types of institutions. While I agree that institution-building may be over, relationships and networking are not. The Presbyterian Church (U.S.A.) is structured around the connections of councils. Those connections do not thrive if they do not create and nurture relationships. In my case, I was a solo pastor in a small church on the far southern edge of the presbytery. My presbytery executive called me one day and offered me a scholarship to attend a continuing education event about small church ministry led by the synod. The content of the event was extremely helpful, but what was really valuable were relationships that were created, some of which I still treasure today.

The presbytery, synod, and General Assembly leaders who feel guilty because connections aren't like they used to be in our denominational mythology would be blessed if they could receive mass forgiveness. The best cure for creeping congregationalism is galloping relationship-building. New types of connections are being created across the PC(USA). These connections are being created as presbyteries and synods find new ways to gather people for conversation and mission. They are being created through social media as various groupings form on Facebook and other sites. Relationships are being formed around new national gatherings on theological and social justice themes. All of these types of building connections will pay off in the denomination's long-term renewal.

4

Spring City Presbyterian Church

Spring City, Tennessee, is a small town of two thousand people, located about an hour south of Knoxville. Spring City Presbyterian Church has been part of the town since 1885. A few years ago there was a painful congregational split, resulting in a membership of only fourteen people. I have a photo of them gathered in the church kitchen around an island that was covered with aluminum foil–covered casserole dishes. The people were all smiles, but one can't help but think of this as a contemporary version of da Vinci's *The Last Supper*.

This story is predictable and too frequent. A congregation shrinks to a small number of older members until it withers away. But this is not that story. The congregation decided, with the help of its stated supply pastor, to focus on youth. Every Saturday they would go out to the Spring City soccer fields and cheer for every player. What boy or girl doesn't want their grandparents cheering them on as they play? The members had Spring City Presbyterian T-shirts made so that there would be no doubt who they were. They designed posters and blew soccer league horns.

People began to notice these wild, cheering Presbyterians. Conversations happened, and families started visiting the church. Membership grew to twenty-five. They had children in the congregation again. They held a blessing of the students as school began. The lot next door came available for purchase for the first time. The session applied for a loan from the Presbytery of East Tennessee. In good, decent, and orderly fashion, the presbytery asked the elders for their plan to pay back the loan. They responded, "We didn't have a plan to get to twenty-five, but we did." Today, with its various community mission activities, Spring City Presbyterian Church has almost sixty participants.

This story does not produce a blueprint for all churches in similar situations. Despite hundreds of books on church growth, there is no universal magic formula to guarantee success. The overall current scene of religion in the United States is less church joining and more following your own spiritual path. But Spring City's experience provides some valuable lessons.

USE THE GIFTS YOU HAVE

Spring City saw an advantage in looking like grandparents. They used their age, which many would see as a drawback, to bring some familial joy to the boys and girls of Spring City. A similar example happened in Indiana with a congregation located in the center of town. When downtown merchants decided they would stay open late on every third Friday of the month, the congregation wanted to be part of it but could not see what they had to contribute. Then they realized there were no public restrooms downtown. The congregation opened its doors (and restrooms) to what became a vital ministry. It grew to include a hospitality and fair-trade ministry. No consultant, no new software, and no capital campaign were needed. They only had to discover the gifts they already had.

SHOW UP

The few members of Spring City Presbyterian Church showed up. Showing up may not seem like a large accomplishment, but it is. As the saying goes, 90 percent of life is showing up. The people of the church didn't just show up at church, they showed up outside the four walls of the building where many people have negative views of a church they see as too judgmental. So, we have to overcome that perception by revealing a different picture of the church.

Spring City transformed the frozen chosen into a bunch of wildly cheering men and women for the sake of the gospel. The payoff was that they changed the congregation's composition. Another photo shows the now larger congregation gathered on a sailboat. Every age group and every racial ethnic group in town are now a part of Spring City. The church features the sailboat photo on its website, and this is what the congregation says about themselves:

> We have a vision of being a sailboat church, the wind filling our sails, the boat moving forward cutting through the waves. We trim the sails as the wind determines and we set out in a spirit of hopeful adventure. It's breathtaking to experience the leading of God's Holy Spirit especially as we "let go and let God" determine our course into the future. We are embracing new opportunities for ministry and we're energized to bring these to fulfillment.[1]

BE WILLING TO RISK

They were willing to risk and willing to be embarrassed. These are the two highest hurdles congregations face when they are staring at the future. I cover risk in other parts of the book, but all the churches discussed took great risks when they moved out of the cocoon of the church and into the community. In

1. http://www.springcityfirstpres.org/get-to-know-us.

the safe space of the church building we have our various security blankets. The order of worship, our pew, our Reformed language, and our mostly beloved fellowship are all the wonderful components of church life. Outside the church we enter a territory where different priorities exist. How many families at those soccer fields were done with religion? So, the first risk is rejection or even hostility.

One of the biggest obstacles I have encountered in conversations with congregations all over the PC(USA) is the fear of embarrassment. I have not yet met a Presbyterian who does not affirm the resurrection of the dead. But they are not so sure about life after embarrassment. It may have to do with our mantra of "being sinfully proud to be a Presbyterian." Spring City, with its clearly identified T-shirts, could have failed miserably. In a small town like Spring City, that failure would generate a widespread conversation. The apostle Paul claims in 1 Corinthians 4:10 that we are fools for Christ's sake. I wonder about that for Presbyterians. I know congregations can have playful picnics and funny skits. People carry on running jokes with each other in Sunday school. But the genuine embarrassment of public failure is a hurdle that keeps many congregations from moving toward their calling. We need a theology of embarrassment that helps us explore our fears, a theology of applied grace that calms the red flush of shame on our faces. We need a Reformed language of providence that will let us see that being a fool for Christ is a calling, not a failing.

The story of Spring City Presbyterian Church is a cautionary tale that small congregations are not necessarily on their deathbed. They do face choices, and they often need outside support and perspective. The connection between the Spring City church and the Presbytery of East Tennessee was vital. The presbytery did not show up on the soccer fields but gave support in many ways and still does today. I have shared this story on many occasions to try to lift the spirits of challenged Presbyterians. Presbytery and congregational leaders all find inspiration in it. While most Presbyterians worship in large congregations, these smaller churches are a very important witness in their community.

The Gatlinburg Presbyterian Church is a small church that took a risk and converted its upper education wing into an overnight retreat center for youth groups that wanted a Smoky Mountains experience. In God's providence, that retreat center is now being used almost weekly as mission teams come to help rebuild homes in Gatlinburg after the disastrous fire in 2016. The John Knox Presbyterian Church in Pasadena was down to twenty in worship on Sundays. A group of young persons who were tired of their various megachurch experiences wanted a church where they could be together. They attended John Knox and felt called to return. The older members saw their sincere interest and took the risk of letting them set the tone for the congregation. That tone included regular doses of bluegrass music despite having a twenty-four-rank organ. The church rebound began, and it now is a healthy church with lots of young families.

QUESTIONS FOR CONSIDERATION

1. When did your congregation take a real risk?
2. What did you learn from that risk-taking experience?
3. What prevents your congregation from taking risks?

5

First Presbyterian Church, Atlanta

We have considered the importance of local congregational worship and connections beyond the congregation to presbytery, synod, and General Assembly councils, all fed by the Presbyterian aquifer. Let's now explore local worship and broader connections in the life and ministry of three additional congregations. I could have shared stories from thousands of congregations, but these three offered an inspirational look at what happens when Reformed people put their words into action.

The Rev. Connie Lee is the partnership minister for First Presbyterian Church of Atlanta and Hillside Presbyterian Church in Decatur, Georgia, bringing those two congregations together in community and international mission opportunities and helping to exhibit what it means to be a connectional church. This was an intentional ministry in which the two congregations said they were going to serve as equal partners, despite their differences. Structure was important. Serving as partners prevents the church with more resources from dominating the project. That does make it quite a bit different. You start from scratch together. You sit around the table and you plan together. You implement those plans together. Congregations that partner

find that they have more things alike than things that are different. Despite size and racial-ethnic composition, these two congregations found they have the same needs, the same desires,
and the same hopes and dreams. One partnership they formed is
with Snapfinger Elementary School. Snapfinger is an elementary
school located in the Hillside community, and both congregations provide tutors. It began as a traditional afterschool tutoring program with students whose parents were able and willing
to drive their child to Hillside where one-on-one tutoring was
provided. But then a couple of nearby elementary schools closed,
and Snapfinger grew from four hundred to nine hundred students. The partnership had to rethink its approach. Now tutors
are paired with students and go to the school when it works for
the student. This again shows the value that Reformed people
place on public education.

The Community Ministries of First Presbyterian Church
of Atlanta is organized around twelve ministries, including the
Hillside partnership. They serve two major groups within the
population: the homeless and the economically disadvantaged.
A few services they provide include a food pantry, a shower
ministry for homeless men, and on Wednesday afternoon they
provide foot care because, as you can imagine, when all your
transportation is on your feet, and your shoes may not fit very
well or you may not have socks, you need foot care. Lee noted
that they can provide foot care thanks to wonderful volunteers.
As you can imagine as well, they rely on hundreds of volunteers
to help.

First Presbyterian of Atlanta houses a transitional center for
homeless women that can serve up to twelve single women,
who can stay between six months to a year. The center focuses
on single homeless women who often have jobs but are sleep-
ing in their cars. They now have a full-time case manager to
help women set goals and save money, and they meet weekly
to see how they are reaching those goals or what changes need
to be made. Their hope and desire are that when the women
leave the Edna Raine Wardlaw Coker Women's Transition
Center, they are actually able to turn the key in their own place.

The connectional and relational nature of First Presbyterian's ministry is seen in the Sunday morning Prayer Breakfast each week. Most of the people who attend the breakfasts are currently homeless. However, it does become a community for those who eventually get their apartments because they come back to get those really good breakfasts. Lee boasts,

> People say we have the very best grits in town! We provide a worship service to give the opportunity for a message, and we work with another local ministry: Walking Power Ministries. They provide people who bring forth the Word and music, and offer a prayer and altar call. Every Sunday morning, we have wonderful volunteers who start the grits, boil the eggs, bake the sausage, bake the biscuits, and serve those things. It is a very nutritious and healthy meal that we serve every Sunday morning: rain, shine, sleet, snow.

The Community Ministry utilizes between seventy and one hundred volunteers weekly. The volunteers provide meals 365 days a year. Volunteers spend the night in the women's transition shelter. They help welcome guests at the many services provided. The use of the term "guests" is intentional. There is no sense of patronizing. The basic Reformed pulse—that because we have received grace from God, we respond in gratitude—is evident.

Lee illustrates this grace-and-gratitude pulse by telling a story about a friend who had a theological insight during her daughters' nighttime prayers. The young daughter who led bedtime prayers with all her heart said her prayers of thanksgiving and included thanks for poor people. The older sister, who had a strong sense of how prayer was to be done, objected that it wasn't right to thank God for people being poor. The wise mother explained that the little sister wasn't thanking God for them being poor'; she was thanking God that they were in her life. It is evident that First Presbyterian, with its beautiful facility amid a beautiful campus, welcomes its guests with equal love and attention.

Another important ministry is the Redemption After Prison program, which works with prisoners as they are released. First

Presbyterian and Hillside partner with the Georgia Justice Project and take families to visit their loved ones in any of the fifty-one counties where they are incarcerated in the state of Georgia. They do this one Saturday a month because persons who have contact with their family are less likely to be incarcerated again. Studies show that strong relationships are more helpful than jobs in keeping people out of prison.[1]

Lee confirms that her church members are truly brothers and sisters to people in their community. They try to be a welcoming community, as is evident in Sunday morning worship services and Sunday school class. The Community Sunday school class is made up of church members, homeless persons, and others involved in the Community Ministries. Every Sunday morning, they come together intentionally to worship together and develop relationships. The difference between guests and church members disappears as dialogue and questions open insights into the Word.

Another pastor at First Presbyterian Church of Atlanta is Greg Allen-Pickett. Greg recently moved to Hastings, Nebraska, and is minister of First Presbyterian Church there, but while he was still in Atlanta we spoke about the effect of the Community Ministries on the volunteers.

> A progressive parishioner named Gayle White, former religion writer for the *Atlanta Journal-Constitution*, works in the church's community breakfast that meets every Sunday morning. The Prayer Breakfast serves our guests: the homeless and urban poor. Gayle told me that every Sunday morning she serves alongside the most conservative member of First Presbyterian Church and a Southern Baptist who would never join this church but would show up for the breakfast. Gayle says they have these theological discussions and debates while elbow deep in dishwater, cleaning the dishes after serving the homeless and urban poor. Gayle

---

1. Danielle Wallace, Chantal Fahmy, et al., "Examining the Role of Familial Support during Prison and after Release on Post-Incarceration Mental Health," *International Journal of Offender Therapy and Comparative Criminology* 60, no. 1 (2014): 3–20.

believes that this is the body of Christ. In this opportunity to serve together, all the other stuff falls away. It isn't that they didn't have theological discussions, but when you are elbow-deep in dishwater, it changes the nature of how you talk to each other.

Allen-Pickett is very passionate about how mission opportunities create relationships.

First Presbyterian Atlanta has six global mission focuses. The church sends a short-term mission group to its mission focus country every year. The folks who go on these trips together are a diverse mix of Presbyterians. They are old, young, liberal, conservative, and moderate. When they go and serve together on a trip like these mission trips, they return as a band of brothers and sisters who are the church. It builds relationships between people who, in a two-thousand-member church, wouldn't ordinarily interact with each other. The opportunity to serve together—whether in Haiti, Kenya, or Brazil, or helping a refugee family set up their apartment in Atlanta—dissolves the other divisive stuff as members focus on what it means to be the body of Christ.

Allen-Pickett told this story about a recent mission trip he led:

> I had some folks come from the more conservative side of the church who had considered leaving the PC(USA) over human sexuality issues, and I had two gay members on the trip. Human sexuality issues didn't come up because we were focused on the belief that every precious child of God was taken care of and was thriving. One person was doing height checks and another doing weight checks in the very same room. They were hugging these kids, loving these kids, and doing what they came to do. One who was ready to leave the denomination over same-sex issues and one who was in a same-sex relationship were working together because ultimately the opportunity to serve together transcends all of that. I've now been on six trips, and I've seen that on every single trip that I've led. This is what it's about.

Two of First Presbyterian's global ministry focuses underscore the value of being the connectional church. One is the La Gonave partnership, a ministry started by First Church in consultation with the Episcopal Diocese of Haiti and focused on the island of La Gonave. The partnership has grown to fifteen to twenty congregations, including some Methodist and Episcopal congregations. An important aspect of this relationship is that First Church first asked questions and admitted it needed partners to meet the challenges presented.

The other newer ministry is with Cuba. First Presbyterian worked with the already established Cuban Ministry Network to begin a partnership with two congregations in Cuba. The Cuban Ministry Network is one of the oldest ministry networks in the PC(USA), an excellent example of congregations and presbyteries working together. Many Presbyterians don't know there is a Reformed church in Cuba. The story of the Cuban church is an inspirational tale of how 20,000 members across the island have banded together to do ministry in significant ways.

How do these ministries create connections? There is an inner circle of about 100 to 150 people across our congregation who connect to the church and to each other because of global missions. In the expanded circle, there are about 250 to 300 people related to global missions who have been on a trip. That's the gold standard, because once you've seen the partnership in action, have spent time receiving the hospitality from their global partners, loving them and being loved by them, you're a changed person, and you can never go back. That is pretty significant. It's a reason for people to be part of the church. That draws people in and connects them to the larger ministry at First Presbyterian and also to the larger body of Christ through global ministry and mission. Some of the people said they became involved because someone personally invited them on a trip. Doing the work of the church is what it means to be a church, expanding the circles. Connections are being created in community ministries, local mission, and global mission.

QUESTIONS FOR CONSIDERATION

1. How do the missions of your congregation create relationships?
2. Could your congregation partner with another congregation to create a more effective ministry?
3. What is your congregation doing in ministry that would encourage you to invite someone to participate?

6

North Avenue Presbyterian Church

I first heard the Rev. Scott Weiner tell the story of the great challenge that came to North Avenue Presbyterian Church of Atlanta in 2015. It is a story that will challenge you about what a congregation can do when confronted with a global evil. The congregation is located within the afternoon shadow of the Bank of America tower. It is down the street from the Midtown branch of Emory University Hospital and one of the largest homeless shelters in Atlanta. The larger story of North Avenue is the connection that a congregation needs to have with its location. That relationship cannot just be a matter of real estate. It should be a driver in how a congregation determines its ministry and mission.

North Avenue has been on the same corner since 1898. Over the years it has had a sense of call to be present in a particular location in this part of the city. It understood that the church is not its buildings; it's the people. It has always felt that God was calling it to be a people from a particular location where they gathered and then were dispersed into the community. That corner of Peachtree Street, the main drag in Atlanta, and North Avenue, which is also a significant thoroughfare, became an important part of its identity. Over the years, the neighborhood around the church changed. Numerous times, probably every ten years or so, the church leadership would consider whether it would make more sense to move closer to its members. Most of its members were coming from a five-mile radius and were commuting into the city. However, its leadership continually felt called to that location even though it was a difficult location in which to do ministry. Over the course of time, the church had begun to see the corner as more of an opportunity than a liability and to think of new ways to reach the local community.

North Avenue began in the 1990s to pray about how to reach people who are significantly different from its membership. The church began to change in significant ways. Now, Sunday participation is about 40 percent multiethnic and multinational. The church changed in a diverse direction and in ways that were challenging and mostly enlightening for the congregation. In the early 2000s it adopted a motto: Becoming Internally Strong in the Things of God, but Externally Focused on the World That God Loves. Everything it does is the mission of Christ in the world. But as the church was thinking about being internally strong and externally focused, a research paper entitled "Hidden in Plain View" came to its attention.

The mayor of Atlanta, Shirley Franklin, produced this report out of a study the city issued that identified the city of Atlanta as a major hub for human trafficking of children, kids under the age of seventeen. In the midst of explaining that this was an issue for metropolitan Atlanta, it highlighted three street corners that were especially problematic for the trafficking of children. One corner was in downtown Atlanta where one might expect. But the other two locations were shocking. One was in the heart of one of the most affluent parts of Atlanta—Buckhead, on the corner of Piedmont and Pharr Road. The third corner was the one that was most shocking to members of North Avenue Presbyterian. It was their very corner, North Avenue and Peachtree Street. Weiner tells how it affected the church:

It was really kind of hard to believe. The report was issued by the mayor's office and reported in the *Atlanta Journal-Constitution*. It was as if, in a very public way, we were called out. It didn't mention our church, of course, but it listed the street names we often talked about as the place where God has called us. It was really like a slap in the face, especially when we were praying about what it means to be externally focused.

We couldn't ignore that report. Well, we could have. We could have just let it pass, but some of our members highlighted that part of the article and put those articles on my desk or handed them to me on a Sunday morning. They didn't say anything. It was clear in their own way they were saying, "What are we going to do?" One of the options was to publicly say we don't see this. We don't believe it. We don't agree with it, because we didn't really see it. However, the report was called "Hidden in Plain View." There were incidents that the police had identified on our own corner even though we hadn't seen them.

A week or ten days after the article had been published and people put the article on my desk, I felt it was important to mention the article in my sermon. I decided to just call it what it was: human trafficking. I made reference to the report and said that I wasn't sure what it meant in reference to the church. However, I was pretty sure that God was calling us to address this issue.

After the Sunday morning services, people met me at the door.

I had been thinking that if anyone was going to be upset that I mentioned this, it would be people in the 11 a.m. worship group. After the service, this group of older women walked right up to me, looked me in the face, and said what I was totally not expecting. "Scott, this is terrible. This is unacceptable. Some of us are widows. We have large homes. It's just us. We have empty rooms. If you need a safe space for kids who are being rescued, let us know. We will open our homes." There were young professionals, young couples, college students, too, who came up saying they were ready to mobilize. "We'll go into the streets in the middle of the night if you want us to." To me it was as if the

Holy Spirit was saying we had to do something through the congregation.

Part of my motivation came from the overwhelming response of the congregation. Their response was inspirational. But also, think about how churched a city like Atlanta is. It must be one of the most churched cities in the United States, which would make it one of the most churched cities in the world. How was something this awful happening in our midst without our seeing it? The Holy Spirit was really speaking to me about our mission and our role, and how this had happened on our watch. This was definitely our issue.

Note here that North Avenue did have a choice. It could do what many congregations do when faced with an overwhelming challenge: count the cost and turn away. It could have said, "Well, our people aren't involved so we don't have to be involved." But North Avenue was preparing itself for this challenge before it knew what the challenge would be. How a congregation connects to a mission is a very important aspect of its connectional life. A congregation has to ask itself, *Are we check writers or hands-on kind of folk?* There is a wide range between those two poles. Not everyone is able to be hands on. Just as First Presbyterian Atlanta moved from clients to guests, reframing and retooling how you connect through mission is important work.

What happened next is a story of connections at every level. After an honest assessment, North Avenue admitted it did not have all the answers. Through Weiner's relationships with other clergy in the city, a coalition was developed. With backing from the presbytery and other denominations, a community-wide meeting of concerned clergy of all types of congregations was convened. North Avenue's neighbor Emory Hospital asked to be a cosponsor. The coalition grew to include business leaders and nonprofit institutions.

Mayor Franklin came and talked with the coalition. She was prophetic for our city. It was wonderful to have a politician who was concerned about such an issue. She didn't have to be concerned about it, but she told us it was important to her. She said to us that, as faith leaders, this was our issue, that our prophets have something to say about this kind of injustice. When the mayor is talking to us as faith leaders, it really is something. She said, "The city needs your leadership and support. Think about the resources you have in your congregation." That resonated with us.

In the end, the coalition of state and federal governments, the nonprofit and business communities, and the faith community have worked together and become a model for some other issues, like public education and affordable housing. It's like a best practice. In the human trafficking arena, a nonprofit called Street Grace was eventually formed to take the grace of God into the streets of Atlanta. GRACE is an acronym for Galvanizing Resources Against Child Exploitation. It took four years to form. This evil didn't just occur overnight, and it's going to take time to eradicate. Over the last number of years this coalition has built capacity to lobby at the state level, changing laws to more severely punish those who exploit children. It works to protect children, to provide resources and funding for the rescue and also the restoration of kids who have been trafficked. As Weiner said,

> This issue of human sex trafficking has made us look more holistically at the community around us. I don't hesitate to say it has been gratifying to see the work that we have been able to accomplish together in the community. My hesitation is because the issue is still so significant and there are still so many kids who are being exploited. When we started, there were very few places where kids who were being rescued could receive the considerable services they would need: emotional, educational, and psychological. Now, though, we've been able to create centers where kids can be rehabilitated. We are seeing kids who are being rescued and restored with a continuum of care and actually finding meaningful employment. That is wonderful to be able to see that come to being.

One of the crucial moments came when a minister told Rev. Weiner that North Avenue was being asked to do what it could. The congregation was freed up when they heard it said that it should do what it could. Any movement is so much bigger than a single congregation. There are others whom the Holy Spirit will bring alongside. Some of those partners will be outside the church. There are a lot of lessons about working with the broader community and working with people who don't see faith exactly the way we do, but who are still working for the common good.

North Avenue's story may seem challenging to your congregation, who may not have that church's contacts or resources. The lesson for me was it is not about size but about vision—the vision that happens when God opens a congregation's eyes to mission right before them. Something else is happening at North Avenue that is worth hearing, the story that is inside the congregation.

Matt Seadore is the executive director of ministry and mission at North Avenue. He shares that the mission North Avenue has been leaning into the hardest over the last few years in the urban area has been figuring out how to create meaningful two-way relationships between the materially poor and non-materially poor. That's been its real big emphasis.

A couple axioms they have learned are these. First, being with is better than doing for. That was an internal shift. One of the dangers it fell into in the "doing for" mindset was it was almost the opposite spectrum with some of the same outcomes of being afraid of the people who were from the streets. In some ways, "doing for" and avoiding both objectified the recipient. The congregation had a lot of well-intentioned objectification of the recipient going on. It didn't even really require anything more than for transactional relationship to occur. You come in. You state that you have a need. I can meet that need, and I decide whether you are worthy of me meeting that need or not. When you begin to build that into your systems, you end up asking the decision-makers to play God with life. They decided to minimize transactional relationships and maximize the actual relationships that were occurring and tried to figure out how to navigate that ground.

North Avenue decided to do three things simultaneously. First they reviewed their system of providing help to people. Instead of seeing themselves as distributors of a big pot of money, they connected with other agencies that believed were helpful in a good way. They did not just make referrals but did all the follow-up to make sure the other agency did its part.

That led to the second step: What would it look like if North Avenue actually welcomed the people who are already here and stopped having ambivalent hospitality? The definition is when you are simultaneously inviting people with one hand and keeping them at arm's length with the other. As soon as North Avenue opened up the doors to membership, the people began to go through those doors really, really quickly. The materially poor may not have a lot of material resources, but many of them have a lot of time. They were very keen to serve and to see their gifts used. As the church did that, people began to experience church a little bit differently when the person handing you your order of service is a materially poor person and not a person with membership of thirty years who looks just like you.

After inviting people into membership and into service, North Avenue took probably the riskiest step. Seadore says, "We pushed pretty hard to say that if we really want to say that we are moving to a new sense of 'we,' we are compelled to invite someone from the materially poor community to serve in our core leadership structure. Two years ago, we did that. We invited a formerly homeless person to serve in our core leadership structure."

Then they started to look at the next part of that goal. What did they offer for people in their congregation who are materially poor? They had a Sunday school class called The Cup. It was under missions, and it was advertised as a class for homeless people. The church realized it probably needed to change the language that was used in the class and the system under which it sits. This class was reframed as part of the adult discipleship program and is now a class that gives voice to street theology rather than being classified as a class for homeless people. The session rotates its elders through that class, giving every elder a turn with that experience.

North Avenue is making that great change of course where walls are brought down and we all stand equal before God and each other. In Geneva, John Calvin set reconciling relationships as a priority of ministry. Like North Avenue, the population of Geneva changed with the great influx of religious refugees from across Europe. It was an ever present mission to build bridges between people.

QUESTIONS FOR CONSIDERATION

1. What are some mission challenges on your church corner?
2. Who would be natural partners in meeting those challenges?
3. What would it take to create relationships as equals with the people you serve outside your congregation?

7

Myers Park Presbyterian Church

A congregation of around five thousand members with a long tradition of service, Myers Park Presbyterian Church sits in a beautiful suburb of Charlotte, North Carolina. The church has chosen to focus its ministry for larger impact. Its associate for mission is Rev. Derek McLeod.

Myers Park has seven global partnerships and twenty-two partnerships around the city. Locally the partnerships are long-term ones, and globally it has been involved with many of its partnerships for a long time as well. In Hungary, they partner with the Debrecen Reformed Great Church. When members of the church visited Hungary several years ago, three thousand immigrants a day were arriving at the Budapest train station. Myers Park became involved in the refugee movement, and they have maintained that connection. That's a new partnership that has been really amazing. They had twenty-eight people going in the summer to run a vacation Bible school for refugees with the Scottish church at its partner church in Hungary.

Like other congregations the ministries are teams of people who are attracted to the ministry, or their friends have brought them in. Myers Park worked hard at creating an internal brand based on Paul's challenge to the church in Corinth. They used part of a phrase, "love builds up" from 1 Corinthians 8:1b, as a kind of gathering connector. Then they organize the ministries into categories. Love builds up a home, a child, a neighborhood, a world. Individuals may be involved in a particular ministry, but they know that ministry exists in a framework or family of ministry. They gather everyone together and have ministries tell their stories to other ministries, so that it's just not everyone doing their own thing.

Rev. McLeod says they encourage the teams to invite others to join because a lot of the ministry is lay driven. It must be because they have so many ministries.

> You have a strong leader, and they have to serve breakfast. If they don't have enough people, they bring their neighbors, bring their friends. Several ministries only happen because members have brought their friends. Some members who left the church when it made a decision around the same-gender marriage issue and affirmed the clergy's ability to perform one on site have remained working in their outreach ministries. They have found room, and hopefully that keeps a door open. It's an interesting model.

These ministries serve as an evangelistic tool. People like to know that their church is doing something. A visitor comes on Sunday and hears about building a home or other help needed. They will go and buy a winter jacket or participate a little bit. But, says McLeod,

> Where the real attraction comes is when their world gets turned upside down. That for me is where you begin to do the work of ministry. The best success I've had with this is when I was working with the thirty- to forty-year-old crowd, called Emerging Leaders. A lot of them are fairly new to the church. Some have been here before college and some after college. What I've had to do is integrate mission experiences into the Sunday adult education lesson. They know that as a part of the church once a month or every two months we do something missionally together. They

want to do it with their families. That's a big change. No one wants to go out there on their own.

One mission we do might be called toxic charity by many. We work with an organization where you just bring brand-new mattresses into people's homes. I kind of held my nose while they did it because it's really not the best model for mission. However, it got really wealthy white people into the homes of a neighborhood that most just drive by. There were people breaking down and sobbing, realizing that there are six people living in a two-bedroom apartment and bedbugs are common. That's when it became deeper than just attraction for many, and they realize they need to be involved in this. Then on Sunday we talk about it. The toxic part is we're just giving you something. We're just showing up in your neighborhood; we're just straight-up Santa Claus giving you something, and we don't know who you are individually. It turned into an incarnational experience. There also were neighbors watching us. When we finished, they called us into a circle, and we prayed together. All of a sudden it became a very different kind of relationship. I actually don't like the term "toxic charity" anymore because it may look toxic when it's not at all, if you are paying attention and being deliberate about relationship, which is the basis of everything you're doing. So yes, I'll say it's attractional and can always be surface until you do a little bit of the work of getting people in.

The community-building continues in the congregation. They talk about their experiences. People realized the experience isn't just the mission to others. The experience is being together, and maybe going for a beer afterward to talk. When they go on a mission trip away, they plan on meeting when they return because they aren't really back until they've unpacked their spirit and their soul. Myers Park is deliberate about creating time for people to invite each other to be a part of their mission experience.

Grier Heights is an economically disadvantaged neighborhood in Charlotte. It is traditionally an African American neighborhood buffered up against the Myers Park neighborhood.

Over several generations this neighborhood has become 80 percent rental, with a lot of government housing. Myers Park supports a school that is 96 percent free or reduced-price lunches. They have independently funded a new teacher mentor. The turnover of new teachers there was really high, but that has stopped now because of having somebody whose job is to coach and mentor the new instructors. They have developed an organization called Cross Roads that has become Myers Park's presence and ministry in Grier Heights. The congregation is involved in afterschool programs and Freedom School in the summer. Fifty people are going in each week as reading buddies. The church helped start Habitat for Humanity in Charlotte. Several years ago, Myers Park told Habitat that it was committed to this neighborhood and are only building in this neighborhood.

The congregation is building a home for a second Muslim family. It is really powerful to be building a home in a black neighborhood for a Muslim family when the political rhetoric was so heated in the fall of 2016. This family invited several children in for tea. They took their shoes off and sat on the carpeted floor with the family, enabling them to experience a different reality than the one the media was showing. These were people they ought to be trusting.

McLeod relays this story about his daughter.

My daughter is fourteen, and she came with me. There is a young Syrian boy also fourteen who had a very treacherous experience crossing from Syria to Turkey. His name is Muhammad. Now when she hears that refugees are terrorists and are taking jobs, etc., she has one word for Muhammad: friend. They are on Instagram together. We just need more experiences together. There were lots of years when there wasn't a lot happening. In Hungary, the team shrank and the trips got a little out of focus, but if it wasn't for that, we would never have been in Budapest when the entire world was looking at Budapest. Relationships always have value. We are a covenantal people. That's an important connection that we can't lose.

One of the connections that comes clear in visiting Myers Park is between people who are doing ministry and their spiritual growth. As seen in other stories in this book, getting people out of their context has multiple benefits. It connects them to a different community. It stretches what they think they can do. It requires them to rethink their own spiritual path. And most importantly, it motivates them to talk about their faith. It would be interesting for Rev. Shawna Bowman from Friendship Church in Chicago to share with Myers Park the storytelling program she is doing with her congregation.

I think the other benefit of these mission connections is it generates the questions that are so important to the Reformed way of life. Why am I privileged? Why has God given me so much and others so little? How literally do I need to take Jesus' admonition, "Truly I tell you, just as you did it to one of the least of these who are members of my family, you did it to me" (Matt. 25:40)?

QUESTIONS FOR CONSIDERATION

1. What stories of mission connect to your faith story?
2. What biblical story helps you understand what you are called to be?
3. What questions pop up in your head as you engage in mission?

8

The Future of Our Connected Life

I want to be very honest in this book, so I must share some reflection on the health and future of the connected life of the Presbyterian Church (U.S.A.). Much has already been written and said about the theological issues that have wounded the relationships in the denomination. Having lived through one attempted church split in my first congregation, I am aware of the pain it causes. Family and longtime friends suddenly eye each other with suspicion. People and pastors who used to enjoy each other's fellowship start avoiding contact. It is a sad story repeated too often in the life of the PC(USA) and in the Reformed family around the world.

That is not the issue on which I wish to focus. The Rev. Shawna Bowman told the truth when she said that those congregations that are in survival mode have no energy left for connections beyond themselves. Survival mode is not limited to small congregations struggling with a lack of resources. For the past twenty-plus years I have had numerous conversations with members and ministers about their future. I have found that it did not matter if I was talking with a congregation of ten members with no indoor plumbing or a large congregation with a fat endowment. They were all uncertain of their future. I checked out that assumption with some of the ministers I interviewed for this book, and they agreed that the focus was too often on what a church lacked, not what it had.

This sense of the imminent demise of a congregation can be focused on the most basic of problems. My mother was a very faithful member of her congregation as long as she was able. I will never forget a conversation I had with her that illustrates this point. We were talking about the midweek program at her church, which included a meal prepared by a staff cook. The problem was that two weeks in a row the meatloaf was not fully cooked. My mother put the blame where it belonged. "If the pastor doesn't get this meatloaf problem fixed, they are going to get rid of him." Forget your seminary education, ministers, and take a culinary class.

Family systems theory entered the church vocabulary largely thanks to Rabbi Edwin Friedman's book *Generation to Generation: Family Process in Church and Synagogue.* Several colleagues and I were fortunate enough to take the yearlong continuing education class that Friedman taught. We then pooled our collective wisdom and held a three-day conference at Montreat Conference Center. I taught a workshop multiple times over the three days. As part of the workshop I asked the class to write on newsprint all of the death statements they heard in their congregations—statements such as, "If we don't get some more youth soon we will need to close the doors," or "If we don't make the sanctuary warmer (or cooler) we will need to close the doors." By the end of the three-day conference the walls of the classroom were covered floor to ceiling with the various death statements.

These statements say many things about how some of our congregations perceive themselves. They are not living, breathing expressions of God's kingdom but fragile, gasping communities of people waiting for God. I want to be clear. These are not deficient believers. Many of them have contextual evidence that their congregation's future is in peril. The local school and the local factories are closed. In farm communities, the rise of mechanized farming means you need fewer people. Fewer people equals smaller congregations. Even in large congregations, the ghost of the former, even larger congregation affects the memories of its members. Like the Hebrew people in Exodus 16, we remember the past as better than it actually was.

The connection a congregation has to its present and future is communicated in subtle ways. I have given this example in ruling elder training around the denomination, and it is usually received with nods of affirmation and laughter until I get to the punch line.

Bill and Sue have been ushers/greeters as long as anyone in the congregation can remember. No one knows how they got elected or when, but they are always there. Their role has allowed them to get to know everyone in the congregation and the vehicles they drive. One warm day, members look out in the parking lot and see a sleek, upscale SUV pull in. They don't recognize the car, so they think, "Visitors with money." The husband and wife get out and reveal they are in their early thirties. "Breeders!" members exclaim. Then the back doors are opened and out comes a couple of young children. "I see some children's sermon kids!" The family enters the church and every Presbyterian who talks to strangers, which is a subset, greets them. After worship, the congregation sends over a bread truck with whole wheat and gluten-free bread to show how grateful they are the family came, I guess because Jesus is the Bread of Life. Now why is all this happening? Because the congregation at some level believes that if the family joins the church, it will save the church. The trouble is that the role of Savior in the Presbyterian Church is already taken by Jesus Christ. The congregation should be sharing that Savior, not seeking it in the family.

The spiritual connectors that should flow through a congregation get cross-wired when the congregation is in survival mode. Symptoms include an increasing lack of commitment, the checking account determining when mission happens, and, as stated before, a drying up of connections to other Presbyterian congregations or even neighboring ones. Using family systems theory, think of it as a family that has a problem and is embarrassed about it. First comes the fear of the neighbors finding out about the problem. Second is the family's suspicion that no other family has ever had this problem. Third is the growing self-definition that they are a problem family. I cannot tell you how many times I have had people describe their congregation to me as a "problem" church.

Here is a dose of reality. All congregations have some problems. A pastor who was reaching the final stretches of a successful construction project shared that now members are arguing over where the coffee pots go. Another with a multimillion-dollar budget said the session was stuck on a fifty-thousand-dollar item. The purpose of the church is to worship God and respond with lives of discipleship, which implies that we are committed to change in our lives. That change happens at different speeds in different lives. The hopefully lively, ever-changing dynamic can only cause some bumping around in a community of faith. Bumping can create relationships or cause problems.

One of the first aspects of congregational life that gets jettisoned when survival mode sets in is the ability to take on risks. Spring City took a risk by going out on that soccer field. John Knox Church in Pasadena took a risk by calling a full-time designated pastor. The risk paid off; the congregation has thrived, and the minister is now fully installed. Both congregations had to get out of their survival thinking and get into possibility thinking.

Here is a chart I have used to explain how this lived out in a congregation:

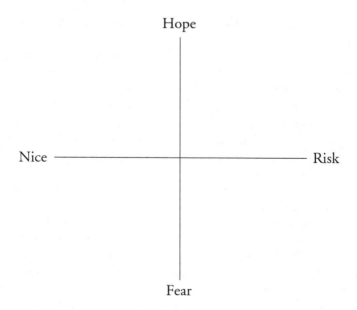

Congregations that are in survival mode get stuck in the nice/fear quadrant. By "nice," I mean the concern that no changes are ever proposed because the congregation does not want to upset anyone—the infamous metaphor of "let's not rock the cradle." When I have presented this chart, I have always issued the caution that I am not advocating that congregational leadership go out and pick a fight for a fight's sake. I am asking that they take an honest look to determine the main operating principle in their congregation.

When I was a teenager, I was elected to be on our church board. The board contained fifty or so well-intended men and women. One of the women was a well-loved and respected doctor who always wore a hat with a feather in it, something like Errol Flynn as Robin Hood. Whenever the minister called for a vote, forty-nine would show their hands in favor or not. Then we would all look at the feather, because its wearer held the only vote that counted. That is typical in a congregation stuck in the nice/fear quadrant. **These congregations need**

connections to help them break patterns and create healthy relationships.

The nice/hope quadrant finds congregations in survival mode living in a Pollyannaish sort of world. They hope the future will just fix itself and they can keep on doing what they have always done. People are generally nice to each other. New babies, usually grandbabies, are welcomed warmly. Grieving families are supported. Members say they are the friendliest church with the best cooks in town. That may be true. A well-known southern pastor once quipped he had never made a pastoral visit to a family with a member facing surgery whose surgeon wasn't the best in the Southeast. The superlatives disconnect it from an honest look about who they are. When someone shows what they look like to others they are frequently shocked and defensive. **These congregations need connections so that they can gain a healthy perspective on their life and ministry.**

The risk/fear quadrant is known by its signs. When I visit a congregation, I notice the signage. If I am in a church with a lot of negative signage, I know the congregation is in risk/fear mode. The signage is just the rules you can read. There are usually many more unwritten norms that you can only find out about by tripping over one. A country congregation had resealed its parking lot. In the process, some signage got displaced. When I visited, I saw that the "Reserved for Pastor" sign that used to hold a parking space was now hanging on the cemetery fence. Not a very encouraging sign. When a congregation gets stuck in this quadrant, the potential for conflict is high. Any change is feared. Any visitors are looked at with suspicion. The presbytery is usually talked about in negative terms. There may be a higher incidence of stress-related illness, especially in leadership. **Connections are needed to both witness to the positive stories from other congregations and to supply leadership with some backing for courageous decisions.**

The hope/risk quadrant is the sweet spot, where a congregation and its leadership are both connected to their theological understanding of hope and their willingness to try new ministry. The congregations in this space are often all too willing to connect with others to share success stories. They have tried and failed at times. But they reflected on the mistakes and learned from them. As Rev. Bowman said about the Friendship Church—they wanted to be a learning lab for the presbytery. Many people understand that the 1001 New Worshiping Communities' project is a vital research and development ministry for the whole denomination. My father would use kitchen leftovers as compost for his garden. He always left a little space in the patch to see what the compost might produce on its own. He was rarely disappointed and learned about new varieties of vegetables. I sense in many PC(USA) congregations a willingness to connect to our resurrection faith, connect to their community, and connect to the denomination as they move out in ministry and mission. These are signs that God is not finished with the Presbyterian Church (U.S.A.). **Healthy connections can inspire hope and encourage congregations to take risk.**

Every congregation circulates through all four of these quadrants. Congregations that live long in the Hope/Risk quadrant often need a rest period to regroup. The goal is to live into the rhythm of these quadrants and know which ones give health and which ones use up energy. I have been using the tool of asset mapping to help congregations get past their risk aversion. That tool is asset mapping.

Community organizers have used asset mapping for many years. Basically, an organizer calls together a community interested in a particular issue and literally maps out where resources can be found and shared. An example would be the Safe Space project that you see in many communities. Many church leaders have been using this approach with congregations much longer than I have, and each one has a slightly different focus.

My focus is to help congregational leadership get past the belief that they have too little to risk losing any of it. This is the scarcity mind-set. Leadership gets focused on dwindling bank accounts and members. They can only see the downslope. But

I try to help them see the real treasure of the church and connect them to their spiritual gifts.

The thing I like most about a congregation is that at any one moment you can have a member who is so new their ears are still wet from baptism and a member who is only one good deed away from Presbyterian sainthood. The huge spectrum in between is where you and I live. There is always somebody to look up to and inspire you to be a better person of faith. Without those people and their gifts, the richest church in the denomination is in poverty.

I ask church leaders to take an inventory of the spiritual assets of their congregations.

Who do people look to in your congregation for

- Spiritual insight?
- Encouragement?
- Practical help?
- Life wisdom?

Who in your congregation

- Struggled and kept the faith?
- Lost hope, lost faith, found hope, found faith?
- Makes your burdens seem lighter?
- Nurtures children?
- Mentors teens?
- Cares for older people?

This list is hardly exhaustive. It does take the bank deposits and building value out of the equation of determining the congregation's value. Congregations that are worried about their future need to connect with their members who have survived multiple wars and recessions. They know about survival and what they discovered about God in that struggle. Does your future seem dismal? Talk with a cancer survivor. They can talk about real fear and how their faith got them through it. Not sure you can change? Connect with people who lost their jobs

and had to reinvent themselves. The tools and experience congregations need are often in their midst if they can only connect to the abundance of spiritual gifts and wisdom.

I believe with all my heart in the connected church. I know
that there have been times of struggle when I didn't want anyone near me, but God usually had other plans. God would
send someone into my sad chapter and help me connect to a
wider world. It gave me perspective on my pain and showed
me possibilities. The challenge we have is that we who are in
congregations where we are not in survival mode should be
able to find some energy to help struggling congregations find
a new path. There is no magic plan to church health. However,
people who have hope and relationships survive struggles better. We have our hope in Jesus Christ. He has modeled for us
the need to be in relationship with those who struggle. I would
say that includes struggling congregations.

I have one last word on this challenge of the future of the
church. People have asked me many times about what gives me
hope about the future of the church. I have various answers,
but I always close with talking about today. Many years ago in
my first call I was with a family in a hospital when the doctor
told them the husband had cancer. The family was shocked, as
you would expect. This wise old doctor then went on to say,
"You know, I could drive out on that busy highway out there
and be killed today, I don't know that won't happen. The only
difference between someone with cancer and anybody else is
they have an inkling of how they might die."

I think congregations in survival mode have an inkling of
how they might die. But they don't know when. So I respond
to people by saying that I care about the future of the church,
but no one really knows what that future will look like. But
I know right now there are homeless people, hungry people,
harmed people, and hopeless people. That condition is right in
front of me, and I am called by Christ to serve. Worrying about
tomorrow only robs me of my energy to serve today. The Presbytery of East Tennessee is struggling for resources like every
other presbytery. Yet because they believe in the future of the

Korean Church of Knoxville, they granted it a large amount of money for a new building. That is a connection that congregation won't ever forget. It is also a model for the congregations of the presbytery.

> As the Foundations of Presbyterian Polity describes, In our own *time*, we affirm that, in the power of the Spirit, the Church is faithful to the mission of Christ as it:
>> Proclaims and hears the Word of God,
>>> responding to the promise of God's new creation in Christ, and
>> all people to participate in that new creation;
>> Administers and receives the Sacraments,
>>> welcoming those who are being engrafted into Christ,
>>> bearing witness to Christ's saving death and resurrection,
>>> anticipating the heavenly banquet that is to come, and
>>> committing itself in the present to solidarity with the marginalized and the hungry; and
>> Nurtures a covenant community of disciples of Christ,
>>> living in the strength of God's promise and
>>> giving itself in service to God's mission.
>>>> (F.-1.0303, emphasis added)

Appendix

Connections

I have included a brief extract from the Committee on the Office of the General Assembly (COGA) summary of a survey of the Presbyterian Church (U.S.A.) in the winter of 2013–2014. I have included it because it gives some statistical data to support some of the results of my own investigation in to the connectional nature of the church. The report is available at http://www.pcusa.org/resource/final-report-church-21st-century/.

I was part of designing the report, working with a team of dedicated and insightful COGA members and the Research Services staff of the Presbyterian Mission Agency. The goal was to hold a mirror and a microphone to the whole church and let people describe who they believe we are. It was one of the projects of which I was the most proud during my service as Stated Clerk.

My comment appears after the extract.

Is It Important to Be Part of the PC(USA)?

One of the first questions we asked was whether it is important to participants that any congregation to which they belong has a relationship with the PC(USA). Of the 2,871 participants answering this question, 56 percent said "yes" and 44 percent said "no" or "I don't know." Participants were also asked if they could explain further.

Yes

Among the 1,598 participants who said that it *is* important, the most frequently reported reason participants cited was the connectional nature of the church, particularly the sense of community and friendships that they enjoy, and the way that this connectionalism leads to pooled resources for more effective ministry (if they referred to the connectional nature in terms of accountability structures or discipline, we counted those as part of the polity/governance theme instead).

What Presbyterians Value about the PC(USA)
Why Presbyterian?

Participants were then asked, "If someone asked you why you are Presbyterian rather than belonging to some other denomination, what would you tell them?" Results are shown in the right-hand column below; 3,052 participants answered this question.

What Presbyterians Value about the PC(USA)

Why It's Important That My Congregation is PC(USA)	Why It's Important That I Am PC(USA)
1. Community/ Connectionalism (30%)	1. Theology (41%)
2. Heritage/Tradition/ Identity (28%)	2. Polity/Governance (29%)
3. Theology (26%)	3. Thinking Church/ Educated Clergy (24%)
4. Polity/Governance (23%)	4. Heritage/Tradition/ Identity (23%)
5. Helping Others (17%)	5. Helping Others (17%)
6. Thinking Church/ Educated Clergy (14%)	6. Inclusive/Welcoming/ Supports Diversity (16%)

Not surprisingly, the themes found in these responses closely mirror those of the previous question, which asked why it's important that their congregation be associated with the denomination. However, the relative importance of these themes (based on the number of people who gave similar responses) shifts as they move from thinking about their congregation to themselves ([The two-columned list above] compares the rank ordering of the top themes from the previous question, shown on the left, with the ordering of the top themes from this question, shown on the right). It's important to note that many of the participants offered multiple reasons.

In the most frequently appearing theme from responses to this question (41 percent), participants said that the theology is the main reason (or one of the main reasons) they are Presbyterian.

About a third (29 percent) say that one of the reasons is polity. Participants especially value the ruling elder/teaching elder balance, the Presbyterian Constitution, and the clear processes for decision making.

About a fourth (24 percent) cited the fact that we are a thinking church: being intentional about thinking and praying through a discernment process when faced with difficult decisions, being open to listening to different voices, and valuing intelligence and education, especially when it comes to having highly educated clergy.

Another fourth (23 percent) mentioned something about personal or denominational identity, heritage, or tradition as a reason why they are Presbyterian. For many, it goes so far back in their family history they cannot imagine not being Presbyterian. For others who may be newer to the denomination, some personal exploration or research has led them to value the rich history of the Presbyterian tradition. And for a few others, it simply means that they were ordained as PC(USA) ministers and have made a historic commitment to the denomination.

In the next largest category, 17 percent said they appreciate that the church helps others and/or provides opportunities for participants to help others, through advocacy, mission work, evangelism, and/or disaster relief/assistance.

The results of the survey underline the importance of the connectional life of the PC(USA). While some in this survey felt disconnected, it would be fair to say they were disconnected over theological and congregation struggles mentioned in this book. It is important to me that you hear their voices too.

The majority of respondents do believe that the connectional nature of our church is important for their congregation. This is good news and gives mid-council and denominational leaders hope for the future. When I look at the two columns covering why it is important that my congregation is connected and why it is important that I am connected to the PC(USA), I see similar trends. Individuals who say that connecting to Reformed theology is important are revealing a value of being connected to a system of theology that is larger than they are. This theology has a five-hundred-year-old history with contributions from around the world. This connection links the individual in time and space to the 80 million people who claim John Calvin as their spiritual ancestor. That is a big family.

Individuals who claim that our polity is important are showing a value for decisions that they have to make with a group. Our committee system may sometimes be slower than a turtle. It does give time for people to give input and for God to give input. Our polity is neither weighed toward anarchy or hierarchy. My Lutheran colleagues like to describe their various councils not by their level in the church hierarchy but by their circle of influence and work. This is a model we should study.

The emphasis on thinking is clear. Having thinking clergy and thinking church members means the freedom to ask. Being able to ask questions about the faith without judgment creates a community—a community that is not afraid to learn together through exploration. A community that is courageously applying faith to context. Where is God calling us to love our neighbors?

Two clear goals covered the theological spectrum: the need for nurture of healthy congregations and active ministry for others.

The need to support congregational health is a key component in the role of a connectional church. Some critics might say it is too inward-looking to be healthy. I would strongly disagree. It is only unhealthy to focus on congregational health if our efforts create inward-focused congregations. There cannot be too many actors in this game. Presbyteries, synods, the General Assembly agencies, large congregations with resources, small congregations with big ideas—all need to dive into this work of building up congregations. The survey gives a hint about what individuals value in the PC(USA). That should help guide the production of resources. But I think the best help will be human resources. In a very popular commercial from a few years ago, the boss calls in his staff and tells them he just had a long talk with an old client. It revealed to him that modern technology helps give good service, but clients need human relationships, too. So he hands out plane tickets to the staff to go talk with their clients. "Where are you going, boss?" one staffer asks. The boss answers, "I am going to go talk with that old client."

I worked as a presbytery leader and on national staff for twenty-two years. I spent lots of time on the road trying to do just that. I know that all mid-council leaders do the same sort of traveling within their presbyteries, as do most of the national staff. We cannot let that diminish. Yes, surely we need a balance of home and work, but we all need to do more than drop into a meeting and fly out. On the other hand, I would also challenge congregations and mid-councils to do more than simply allocate five minutes for a visiting connectional speaker from a mid-council or national staff at their meetings. Create dialogue groups for them. I learned the most about what was going on in the denomination in fellowship halls over fried chicken and pea salad. Let's connect.

The other emphasis is helping others and advocating for social justice. There is a clear biblical mandate to do so. The recent elections have taught me that poverty knows no geographic boundary. As a church with much privilege, we have an obligation to fight for those with no privilege, at both the community level and in national arenas. No congregation can fight these fights alone. Connection must happen to serve the need and create the change. One of the clear messages I received in these interviews and of this survey is that social justice work is not the killer of denominations. It is a strong priority because we are a church. We might debate methodology, but there is little debate on what we are called to do.

> The Church has been and is even now sent into the world by Jesus Christ to bear that testimony to others. The Church bears witness in word and work that in Christ the new creation has begun, and that God who creates life also frees those in bondage, forgives sin, reconciles brokenness, makes all things new, and is still at work in the world.
> (Foundations of Polity, F-1.0301d)

This is who we are in the twenty-first century. We are a connected church striving to be more connected to live out the best of Reformed traditions and theology, our call to serve, and our call to be connected to each other in ministry and mission.